Stu

The С....

by Moses Maimonides

STUDENT'S COMPANION to

The Guide of the Perplexed

by Moses Maimonides

BEN ZION KATZ, MD

URIM PUBLICATIONS

KTAV PUBLISHING

Jerusalem • New York

Student's Companion to *The Guide of the Perplexed* by
Moses Maimonides
by Ben Zion Katz
Series: *Student's Companion to Jewish Studies*

Copyright © 2021 Ben Zion Katz

Typeset by Ariel Walden

Printed in USA

First Edition

ISBN 978-1-60280-429-6

Urim Publications
P.O. Box 52287,
Jerusalem 9152102 Israel
www.UrimPublications.com

KTAV Publishing
527 Empire Blvd.
Brooklyn, NY 11225
www.ktav.com

Library of Congress Cataloging-in-Publications Data in progress

This book is dedicated to our mother
who filled our home with love and *Yiddishkeit*

ESTHER IDA KATZ
Ester Chayah bat Chanoch ve Malya,

may she live and be well

Contents

Introduction

THERE HAS BEEN A NEED FOR A STUDENT'S commentary in English to Moses Maimonides' philosophical masterpiece *The Guide of the Perplexed* (henceforth the "Guide") since it was first translated into English over a century ago.[1] I am not a professional philosopher, nor do I read Judeo-Arabic. Nevertheless, after decades of (re)reading the *Guide* as well as books and articles written by Maimonides scholars and commentators (mainly in English), I have written a personal, somewhat idiosyncratic, and what I hope will be helpful student's companion to the *Guide*; in that spirit I have kept chapter footnotes to a relative minimum.

The best English translation of the *Guide* to date is that of Shlomo Pines,[2] and all references to the *Guide*

---

1. M Friedlander. *The Guide for the Perplexed by Moses Maimonides.* Second edition. 1904. Routledge & Kegan Paul. Dover edition, 1956.

2. S Pines. *The Guide of the Perplexed: Moses Maimonides.* University of Chicago Press. Chicago and London, 1963. For an argument for the superiority of Pines' English translation see M Fox, *Interpreting Maimonides: Studies*

will be to that edition (cited as "Pines, p." followed by the page number). Friedlander's earlier translation is generally not as precise, although his introduction and notes are quite useful.[3] Shlomo Pines' introduction to the sources used by Maimonides in the *Guide* is also helpful.[4] The introductory essay in the Pines translation, by the noted scholar Leo Strauss, is abstruse.[5]

There are many excellent biographies of Maimonides available, both as independent works as well as parts of longer works on Maimonides' life and thought. For example, reliable, brief biographies of Maimonides can be found in the first chapters of Herbert A Davidson's *Moses Maimonides: The Man and His* Works (Oxford 2005) and in Moshe Halbertal's *Maimonides: Life and Thought* (translated by Joel Linsider, Princeton 2014).

In this short work I will present a chapter by chap-

in Methodology, Metaphysics and Moral Philosophy. University of Chicago Press, Chicago and London, 1990, pp. 47–54.

3. Friedlander, *op. cit.* "Analysis of the Guide for the Perplexed," pp. xxxix–lix.

4. Pines, *op. cit.*, "Translator's Introduction: The Philosophic Sources of the Guide of the Perplexed," pp. lvii–cxxxiv.

5. Fox, *op. cit.*, p. 55 "It . . . [is] regrettable that Strauss has chosen to write interpretations that are as esoteric as the *Guide* itself." See also HA Davidson, *Moses Maimonides: The Man and His Works*. Oxford, 2005, pp. 393–402.

ter synthesis of my understanding of the structure and interpretation of the *Guide* based on a selection of the scholarly literature on the *Guide* that I have found useful and convincing. My reading will be a middle path, an Aristotelian golden mean, if you will, between what Halbertal called the conservative and philosophical readings of the *Guide*.[6]

---

6. M Halbertal, *Maimonides: Life and Thought.* Translated by J Linsider, Princeton University Press, Princeton and Oxford, 2014, p. 279.

Outline of the Life and Works of Moses Maimonides, The RAMBAM

March 30, (14 Nissan) 1135: Traditional date of birth, in Cordova, Spain (although some put his year of birth anywhere from 1131–1138)

1148: Maimonides' family leaves Cordoba, likely due to persecution

1148–1158: While still without a permanent home, Maimonides writes several minor works (one on the calendar [which was later incorporated into the *Yad Hachazakah/Mishnah Torah* – see below], one on logic) and begins his first great work, the *Commentary on the Mishnah*.

1160: Family settles for a while in Fez, Morocco. David, Maimonides' younger brother, supports Maimonides' scholarship while working as a jeweler. Maimonides writes one of his famous epistles to a Jewish community in distress, urging tolerance of the nonobservant.

1165: Persecution reaches Morocco; Maimonides' family leaves for Israel.

1166: Family settles in Egypt, eventually establishing a permanent home in Fostat (old Cairo), the capital of Egypt at the time.

1168: Maimonides publishes his first notable work, the *Commentary on the Mishnah*, in whose introduction, and scattered throughout, he discusses important theological and philosophical issues with which he will continue to wrestle for the rest of his life.

1169: Begins work on his second masterpiece, The *Yad Hachazakah*, literally, the strong arm (cf. Deut. 34:12, the last verse of the Torah, where this expression is used in association with Moses). The letters of the word *yad* in Hebrew add up to 14 and thus the title is also an allusion to the book's division of Jewish law into 14 categories. The work is also called the *Mishnah Torah* (companion or supplement to the Torah, a name upon which Maimonides' critics pounced). This work, the only one of his written in Hebrew, was the first code of Jewish law ever published; it included *all* Jewish law, including laws no longer operative without a Temple in Jerusalem, such as sacrifices, and was the first collection of Jewish law in a millennium. Despite the magnitude of this achievement, the book evoked controversy because of its title (thought to be haughty) and Introduction (in which Maimonides states that no other Jewish law book need be consulted besides his Mishnah Torah and the Bible).

1172: Maimonides writes another epistle, this one to the Yemenite Jewish community forced to undergo conversion to Islam, in which he disproves the thesis of a rabbinic contemporary who argued that practicing

Judaism in secret was worse than not practicing it at all. In gratitude, Yemenite Jews to this day generally follow Maimonides' opinions regarding Jewish law (*halachah*, literally, the way to walk) and added an allusion to the Rambam in their *kaddish* (memorial prayer).

1173–4: Maimonides' father and brother die within a short time of each other. Rambam, who by this time was recognized as the head of the entire Moslem Jewish community (he likely served as the *ras al Yahud* – leader of the Jews – for a few years around this time) would not support himself as such. Therefore, he takes up the practice of medicine and is appointed a court physician to the sultan.

1180: Completes the *Mishnah Torah*, or *Yad Hachazakah*.

1183: Marries and has two children, a daughter who died in infancy and a son, Abraham. Abraham reportedly resembled his father in many ways but lacked his intellectual stature. He did write a commentary on Genesis and Exodus (see e.g., footnote 19) and responsa.

1185: Joseph ben Judah Ibn Simon, a young Jewish scholar, seeks out Rambam as a mentor. He becomes Rambam's favorite pupil and a lifelong friend.

1190: Maimonides completes his third great work, *The Guide of the Perplexed*. It is dedicated to his best student, Joseph ben Judah Ibn Simon. Written in Judeo-Arabic, it was first translated into Hebrew by the famous medieval poet and translator, Samuel Ibn Tibbon. Ibn Tibbon had to invent Hebrew philosophical vocabulary in order to translate the *Guide*, and consulted Maimonides himself on difficult passages; because of that, even today Ibn Tibbon's translation is often consulted (see for example Book Three chapter 51), especially if there are difficulties in the Arabic text. Ibn Tibbon wished to visit Maimonides to discuss some aspects of the translation in person. Maimonides kept dissuading him from such a visit, ostensibly because Maimonides claimed to be too busy (see below), but in reality likely because it would involve travel by ship and Rambam's brother had died on just such a voyage. Ibn Tibbon finally set out on his journey, arriving two weeks after Rambam passed away. The *Guide* was also translated into Latin and circulated all over Europe as well as the Middle East; Rambam remains one of the few medieval Jews whose work influenced many leading Catholic theologians and philosophers, notably Thomas Aquinas. The *Guide* is one of the most widely read medieval philosophic texts. It evoked even more controversy than the *Mishnah Torah*.

1190–1204: The last years of Maimonides' life were devoted almost exclusively to medicine. In one letter, Rambam described how busy he was, with only a bit of time for study on the Sabbath, although this might be an exaggeration, as mentioned above (to dissuade Ibn Tibbon from an ocean voyage). He wrote 10 medical treatises during this time.

December 13 (20 Tevet) 1204: Dies a few months shy of what would probably have been his 70th birthday. He is buried in Tiberias and was mourned both by Jews and Moslems for the traditional 30 days (see e.g., Numbers 20:29 and Deut. 34:8, in which Israelites mourn the deaths of Aaron and Moses respectively, each for 30 days).

Plan of *The Guide of the Perplexed*

MAIMONIDES BEGINS THE *GUIDE* WITH A Letter to his favorite pupil, Joseph ben Judah ibn Simon, for whom the *Guide* was written. The *Guide* proper then follows, and it is divided into three books. Each book has an introduction; the introduction to the first book contains both an introduction to Book One as well as an introduction to the *Guide* as a whole.

The main purpose of Book One is to prove that God is not corporeal. The book is divided into two main sections. In the first 68 chapters, Maimonides' main focus (in chapters 1–16, 18–25, 28–30, 36–49, 65–67) is to free us "from the misleading effects of human language . . . that distorts our conception of God"[7] by explaining figuratively the anthropomorphisms found throughout the Bible, which led to the misconception of His corporeality. Along the way, Maimonides includes a digression (chapter 17), two

---

7. M Goodman. *Maimonides and the Book that Changed Judaism: Secrets of the Guide for the Perplexed*. Jewish Publication Society, Philadelphia, 2015, p. 189.

philosophical interludes (chapters 26–27 and 31–35), a discussion of the attributes of God to the extent that they can be known (chapters 50–60), and a section (chapters 61–64) on the significance of the Divine Names. Chapter 68 concludes the first part of Book One. As will be shown, some of the figurative explanations of terms found in this first section of Book One (e.g., ascending and descending) are important for grasping ideas that Maimonides presents in Books Two and Three (e.g., prophecy).

The second part of Book One, chapters 69–76, is a polemic against a major branch of Islamic philosophy known as the Kalam or Mutakallimun, to which Sadia Gaon adhered;[8] in this second part of Book One there is a single chapter (chapter 70) which again discusses the figurative interpretation of a Biblical term.

Book Two begins with proofs of the existence of God (chapters 1 and 2) and then, following a few preparatory chapters (3–12), discusses the major, related topics of creation (chapters 13–31) and prophecy (chapters 32–48).

The major topics of Book Three are Divine pro-

---

8. J Obermann, L Ginzberg, HA Wolfson, eds. Yale Judaica Series. Volume I: *Saadia Gaon: The Book of Beliefs and Opinions;* Translated by S Rosenblatt. Yale University Press, New Haven and London, 1948 and 1976.

vidence (chapters 9–25) and the purpose of the commandments (chapters 26–49). This book begins with some preparatory material (chapters 1–8) and concludes with an epilog (chapters 50–54).

Detailed Outline of
The Guide of the Perplexed

I. BOOK ONE: The Nature of God

    A. Explanation of anthropomorphic terminology in the Bible (chapters 1–16, 18–25, 28–30, 36–49, 65–67, and 70). Maimonides explains that such language is meant figuratively and not literally, and he often proves this by showing that many times the same term is used figuratively even when not referring to God.

    B. Discussions of the nature of "divine science" (metaphysics, or philosophy)

        1. It should be withheld from the multitude (chapter 17)

        2. Limitations of human comprehension (chapters 31–32) and how they can be overcome, to some degree, by studying "natural science" (what we call today science) as a prelude to divine science (chapters 33–34)

        3. Despite the limitations of the masses, everyone needs to (at least) understand God's incorporeality (chapter 35).

C. The nature of angels (chapters 43 and 49)

D. Differences between God and everything else (chapters 50–53 and 68); e.g., He cannot be defined and motion does not apply to Him (chapter 52).

E. The meaning of the attributes of God (chapters 54–60), which often must be stated in the negative (chapters 58 and 59).

F. The meaning of the names of God (chapters 61–64).

G. God – The first cause of the philosophers (chapter 69).

H. Errors in the philosophy of the Mutakallimun (chapters 71–76), Moslem theologians, many of whom believed that everything happens because God wills it. Maimonides abhorred this philosophy (which might on the surface appear to be a proper philosophy for a religious individual) because without causality, Maimonides cannot use a first cause proof for God's existence.

II. BOOK TWO: The Nature of the World, Torah and Prophecy

A. More on God, angels and related matters (e.g., the spheres – medieval astronomy – chapters 1–12).

B. Creation in time, as opposed to the eternal universe of Aristotle (chapters 13–31) (*maaseh bereshit*).

   1. Maimonides was not against the idea of an unchanging eternal universe because it seemed to contradict the Bible, but rather because an unchanging universe does not allow for reward and punishment or miracles. He is not opposed to the idea of a world with no end (chapters 27–29), nor necessarily to the concept of eternal "matter" co-existing with God (chapters 13 and 25).

   2. The institution of the Sabbath commemorates creation (chapter 31).

C. Prophecy (chapters 32–48)

   1. God does not really choose prophets; men strive towards prophecy by achieving perfection through training (chapter 32).

   2. Prophecy is the reception of an overflow of knowledge from God by individuals who have achieved perfection of the body (chapter 36).

   3. Differences between philosophers (overflow to the rational faculty) vs. prophets (overflow to the rational and imaginative faculties) (chapter 37).

4. Moses was the greatest prophet (chapter 39; this is one of Maimonides' fundamentals of Judaism) because his prophecy was mediated solely via his intellect. Moses is thus a unique, philosophical prophet.

5. The purpose of the Torah is to perfect the individual and society (chapters 39 and 40).

6. Prophets and the Torah often speak in parables or hyperbole (chapters 43, 47 and 48) because they (except for Moses) communicated with God also via their imagination.

III. BOOK THREE: The purpose of the Torah/ Divine Providence/ Man's Ultimate Goal

A. The vision of Ezekiel (*maaseh merkavah*); more on metaphysics, figurative expressions, and prophecy (chapters 1–7).

B. Moral and religious matters (chapters 8–9).

C. The nature of evil (chapters 10–12).

D. A perspective on the meaning of life (chapters 13–14; equates angels with the celestial spheres of medieval astronomy in chapter 13).

E. Divine providence and free will (chapters 15–21).

1. Explains the old conundrum of, "Can God make a rock too heavy for Him to lift?" as a contradiction in terms (although Maimonides doesn't use this example; chapter 15).

2. God watches over people, not animals (chapter 17).

3. Free will vs. omniscience (chapter 20). Maimonides argues that God's knowledge is different from ours (chapter 21), thus helping to reconcile the concepts of Divine omniscience and human free will.

F. Trials and tribulations (chapters 22–24).

1. The story of Job (chapters 22–23); shows how little we understand of God.

2. The meaning of human trials and tribulations (chapter 24): to let people know what they ought to do (in certain circumstances) or should believe.

G. Differences between the actions of man and God (chapter 25); God only wills what is possible in the universe as He designed it; thus, even He can't make 2 + 2 = 5.

H. The philosophy of Torah (chapters 26–49)

1. All Torah laws have a purpose (chapter 26)

2. The purpose(s) of various Torah laws

   a. To put an end to idolatry (chapters 29–31, 37, 45, 46, 48)

   b. To control passions (chapters 33–34, 49)

3. Fourteen categories of Law (chapters 35–49); note that these do not match the 14 divisions in the *Yad Hachazakah*.

   a. Chapter 41 discusses punishment and different types of transgressors.

   b. Chapter 43 discusses the holidays and *midrashim* (homiletical interpretations of Scripture).

   c. Chapter 45 discusses the temple in Jerusalem.

   d. Chapter 49 discusses circumcision.

I. Epilogue and Summation (chapters 50–54)

   1. The metaphor of the king in his palace (chapter 51)

   2. Maimonides concludes his *magnum opus* as it began, with the definition of a few terms (e.g., *chochmah* – knowledge/ wisdom [of God]).

Maimonides' Introduction to
The Guide of the Perplexed

MAIMONIDES' INTRODUCTION TO THE *GUIDE* is critical,[9] because in it Maimonides delineates his methodology. Before the Introduction is a preface (Pines, pp. 3–4), in which Maimonides explains that the book is written for his best student, Joseph ben Judah ibn Simon, who, upon studying philosophy, became perplexed. Joseph could not continue studying personally with Maimonides, so Maimonides wrote the *Guide* for him. The *Guide* therefore is not for everybody, as Maimonides makes clear many times throughout the work, beginning here in the Introduction (Pines, pp. 5, 10 and 18). Writing the book (ostensibly) for a single, perplexed, Jewish student also served to technically sidestep the rabbinic prohibition of disseminating certain sensitive religious teachings to the masses (see Book One, chapter 17).

---

9. This was first made clear to me by Dr. Albert Baumgarten.

The first part of the Introduction is an introduction to Book One (Pines, pp. 5–17). Here Maimonides defines several terms: One is *equi-vocal*, meaning that a word can have two meanings, often entirely different from each other; this usually occurs when the word is used to refer both to God (in one way) as well as to people (in another way); many times the word, when it applies to God, will be an anthropomorphism. The second term is *amphibolous*, which Maimonides defines as a word that might be equi-vocal or uni-vocal (having one meaning). Maimonides also implies that there are deep philosophical truths in the Bible, and he introduces here the concepts of "The account of the beginning, [which] is identical with natural science [what we call today science] and the account of the chariot [which is identical with] divine science [what we call today philosophy]" (Pines, p. 6); see also Book One, chapter 17.

The second part of the Introduction is an Introduction to the entire Guide. Here Maimonides explains his methodology (Pines, pp. 17–20). Maimonides begins by listing seven categories of errors, the last three of which are crucial to understanding the *Guide*. The fifth type of error is an intentional (over-) simplification made by the author for explanatory purposes, which by definition is not really an error. The sixth type of error is an actual mistake made by the author unintentionally. The seventh type of error is a subtle but intentional contradiction made by the author to conceal his true belief. According to Maimonides, all errors in the *Guide* are of the fifth or seventh variety. Aside from the bold assertion of Maimonides that his book has no real errors, he is telling the careful, sophisticated reader to be alert for subtle contradictions in order that the reader be able to uncover Maimonides' true beliefs. We will make use of this reasoning when discussing Maimonides' views of creation in the relevant chapters of Book Two.

Book One

(1)

As already mentioned, the first 68 chapters of Book One prove that God is not corporeal. While seeming trivial to monotheists today, this was a major accomplishment in the twelfth century, and did receive some push-back from Maimonides' critics when he asserted that those with misconceptions about God will have no share in the world to come.[10] Maimonides expended much effort in this endeavor because he believed that misconceptions about God were worse than idolatry. In this overview of the first part of Book

---

10. Compare HA Wolfson, *The Philosophy of the Kalam*. Harvard University Press. Cambridge, MA and London, 1976, pp. 97–111. Rambam states in the *Mishnah Torah* that whoever believes God is a body has no share in the World to Come (*Hilchot Teshuvah,* Laws of Repentance, 3:7). For criticism of this approach, see the comments of Rabbi Abraham ben David of Posquieres (Rabad, ca. 1125–1198) *ad. loc.* where he states (paraphrasing): Why do you call them [previous generations of great piety] heretics? Previous individuals greater and better than you (literally "him") were misled by confusing statements found in Scripture and recorded in legends (*aggadot*).

One, I will highlight the key parts of Maimonides' argumentation, explain terms and concepts that require clarification and discuss some of the detours which Maimonides takes along the way.

The first 6 chapters of Book One are *lexicographic*, to use Strauss' term (Pines, pp. xxiv–xxv), or what may also be called "definitional." Here Maimonides reinterprets some of the troubling terms used in the Bible to describe God that misled the unsophisticated into believing that God has a body, although one "more resplendent than ... themselves, and ... composed ... not [of] flesh and blood" (Pines, p. 21). Maimonides explains, for example, that when the Bible says, "Let us make man in our image" (Gen. 1:26), the word "image" refers to "intellect" (Pines, p. 22). In chapter 2, Maimonides mentions the Aramaic translation of the Bible by Onkelos for the first time.[11] In addition, he mentions for the first time the notion of "the (active) intellect that God made overflow into man" (Pines, p. 24). This concept will be discussed in greater depth in

---

11. Onkelos the proselyte is the traditional author of the standard Aramaic translation of the Torah from Hebrew, which was used for centuries by Babylonian Jewry, for whom Hebrew was no longer their primary language. Maimonides has more to say about Onkelos in Book One, chapter 21.

Book Two, chapter 12. Maimonides continues that it is because of this overflow of God's intellect into man that man is said to be created in God's image (and which allows the inanimate – God, or at least His intellect – to somehow, very indirectly (see Book One, chapters 51–60), interact and communicate with the animate – humanity). Also in chapter 2, Maimonides explains that when Adam and Eve were punished in the garden of Eden after eating from the tree of knowledge, they already knew the difference between "truth and falsehood" (Pines, p. 24) because some of God's intellect had already flowed into them. Their punishment was the new ability to distinguish fine from bad – in other words, they were taught esthetics, not morality. Maimonides proves this by explaining how fitting Eve's punishment was – for coveting a beautiful tree (Gen. 3:6) she (and man) would henceforth forever be distracted by matters of esthetics.

In chapter 5, Maimonides presents for the first time the notion that philosophers must work on both their "soul" (mind) by "training in the sciences" as well as their body by eliminating unnecessary "desires and cravings" (Pines, p. 29). Maimonides will revisit this key concept in more detail in Book Three, chapter 27, when he discusses the purpose of Torah, which is also to perfect the body (and society) so that the mind can then be perfected by study.

In chapter 7, Rambam[12] discusses the equi-vocal term *yalad*, which means, when applied to people, its literal sense of "gave birth to [offspring]," but when applied to God, means, in a figurative sense "brought forth [the natural order]," e.g., mountains or vegetation. Maimonides then goes off on a slight digression, informing us (based on a midrash found in the Talmud [*Eruvin* 18b] and in Genesis Rabah 24:6) that the children born to Adam before Shet (i.e., Cain and Abel) were not completely human. The major medieval Jewish commentators on the *Guide* (Efodi,[13] Shem Tov[14] and Abrabanel[15]) consequently understood Rambam

---

12. For stylistic reasons, I will alternate between Maimon-ides, which means son of Maimon in Greek and the Hebrew acronym RaMBaM, which similarly means **R**abbi **M**oshe **b**en (son of) **M**aimon.

13. Profiat Duran, known as Efodi, ca 1350–ca 1415. His Hebrew commentary was printed along with the Hebrew translation of the *Guide* by Shmuel Ibn Tibbon in *Sefer Moreh Nevuchim LeHaRambam*, Vilna 1904, reprinted Jerusalem 1960 and 2004.

14. Shem Tov ben Joseph, 15th century. His Hebrew commentary was also printed along with the Hebrew translation of the *Guide* by Shmuel Ibn Tibbon, in *Sefer Moreh Nevuchim LeHaRambam*, Vilna 1904, reprinted Jerusalem 1960 and 2004.

15. Don Isaac Abravanel, 1437–1508. His Hebrew commentary on the *Guide* too was printed along with the Hebrew translation of the *Guide* by Shmuel

as saying that the entire Cain and Abel story (Gen. 4) is an allegory. The likely reason they felt Maimonides did not take the Cain and Abel story literally is that Cain has mistaken notions about God (e.g., believing that His knowledge was not all-encompassing, as in Gen. 4:9 when Cain attempts to lie to God) despite the fact that Cain speaks with God; if the story were factually true, Maimonides would be hard-pressed to explain how a prophet (who by definition "speaks" with God) could have such a major misconception about Him.[16] The Rambam's understanding of prophecy will be a major topic of Book Two.

Chapters 8–16 continue in the lexicographic/definitional vein. Aside from convincing people that God is not corporeal, Maimonides begins his philosophical program in some of these definitional chapters. For example, in chapter 10, Maimonides discusses the concept of God ascending and descending. Maimonides explains that when referring to God, "descends" means that God allows man to have "some . . . knowledge deriving from Him" (Pines, p. 36) and that "as-

---

Ibn Tibbon in *Sefer Moreh Nevuchim LeHaRambam*, Vilna 1904, reprinted Jerusalem 1960 and 2004.

16. See Marc B Shapiro, Seforim blog 4/7/11, accessed 4/8/11.

cends" means that Divine communication stops (cf. Gen. 17:22, cited by Maimonides in this chapter). This has obvious implications for understanding God's descent upon Mount Sinai (cf. Exodus 19:20, again a verse quoted by Maimonides in this chapter). Some of these ideas are further developed in chapters 15, 18 and 27.[17] Maimonides will also expand upon these ideas when he discusses prophecy in Book Two. Chapter 11 discusses God's permanence, changelessness and stability, denoted by the equi-vocal term "sitting." In chapter 16 Maimonides mentions God as "the first principle" (Pines, p. 42) for the first time. This idea is further developed in Book One, chapter 69, and Book Two, chapters 1 and 2.

Chapter 17 discusses the notion that some of what is discussed in the *Guide* should not be publicized or spelled out in too much detail. This idea will come up again in the *Guide* and there will be more to say about it later. For now, it is important to understand some of the terms and concepts that are introduced in this chapter.

Natural science roughly corresponds to what we

---

17. I thank my brother, Rabbi Jeffrey (Shalom) Katz for highlighting these insights for me.

today would call science – i.e., the understanding of nature and the universe. Rambam used this term interchangeably with the phrase *maaseh bereshit* – the work (science) of creation (as recounted in Gen. 1–2). In contrast, "Divine science" or *maaseh merkavah* – literally the work (science) of the (celestial) chariot (referring to Ezekiel 1; see the discussion at the beginning of Book Three) – refers to metaphysics (what we refer to as philosophy or theology).

Another concept to which Maimonides refers in this chapter is the Aristotelian idea that the universe is divided into the sublunar world, i.e., our world ("below the moon") which is made of terrestrial matter that contains the four terrestrial "elements" (earth, air, fire and water), has form (shape) and is corruptible/changeable, as opposed to the rest of the (supralunar) universe which is made up of a different, fifth element (the "quintessence") that is incorruptible and unchanging.[18] A second concept is the Platonic idea of *particularization*, which refers to the consideration of particular examples of an idealized

18. This idea, of course, is not compatible with modern physics, which assumes that matter and the laws of nature are constant throughout the universe. See also D Wootton, *The Invention of Science: A new history of the scientific revolution.* Harper Collins, NY, 2015, p. 69.

concept. According to Plato we cannot imagine the general concept of "chair," only particular examples of chairs. (This notion will reappear in Book One, chapter 74.) Thus the concept "chair" is supralunar and unchangeable; in contrast, all chairs with which we are familiar (the "sublunar" ones in the real world) are particular examples of chairs that will eventually fall apart ("decay").

Chapters 18–25 are again lexicographic/definitional. In chapter 21 Rambam cites and again discusses the ancient Aramaic translation of the Bible by Onkelos (first mentioned above in chapter 2). Because Onkelos rarely translated an anthropomorphism literally, Rambam favors the translation of Onkelos and cites it frequently throughout the *Guide*; see especially Rambam's comments in Book One, chapters 27 and 28.

Chapters 26 and 27 provide one of the first significant philosophical digressions of the *Guide*. In chapter 26 Maimonides introduces a concept very important for his thesis that the Torah speaks in the language of man (Hebrew: *dibrah Torah bilshon beney adam*; Latin: *scriptora humana loquitor*). This chapter also makes reference to the Aristotelian concept of an *accident*, or non-essential characteristic (e.g., color).

Chapter 27 again extols the virtues of Onkelos' translation of the Bible and introduces some of the concepts related to prophecy and angels that Maimonides will return to later in Book One (e.g., chapter 49) and especially in Book Two.

Chapters 28–30 are again lexicographic/definitional. Chapter 28 once more explicitly extols Onkelos for "the rejection of the doctrine of the corporeality of God" (Pines, p. 60), and builds upon Onkelos' translation of God's throne (in Exodus 17:16) as "His glory," to mean created light.[19] Maimonides continues along this vein to interpret the verse in Exodus (24:10) which describes Moses, Aaron and the elders "seeing" God as *comprehending* the fact that "first matter" (symbolized by the sapphire stone in Exodus 24:10) "derives from Him" (Pines, p. 61; see Maimonides' major discussion of creation in Book Two and his discussion of the sapphire stone in Ezekiel's vision at the beginning of Book Three). Chapter 30 ends with a discussion of the terms "eating" and "water" that, at times in certain Biblical books (e.g., Eccle-

19. See, not surprisingly, the comments of Rabbi Abraham the son of the Rambam on Exodus 16:7 in *Peirush Rabbeinu Avraham ben HaRambam Z"L al Bereshit ve-Shemot,* translated by EY Weisenberg. Honig & Sons, London, 1959.

42

siastes/Kohelet) apply to knowledge, for which the righteous strive (as if for food or water). This all has direct implications for understanding Exodus 24:11, which relates how after "seeing" God, Moses, Aaron, Nadav, Avihu and 70 elders "ate and drank" (i.e., comprehended).

Chapters 31–35 are a more substantial philosophical digression; perhaps they are placed here because they follow Maimonides' discussion of righteous, knowledgeable men at the end of chapter 30. In chapter 31, Maimonides discusses the limits of understanding. He distinguishes mathematics, which has no perplexity because everything can be proven,[20] from natural science, which has very few perplexities because most things related to natural science are provable, and from divine science (metaphysics), which by its nature is perplexing. Maimonides warns about perpetuating false beliefs based on "habit and upbringing" (Pines, p. 67). In chapter 32, Maimonides refers to the famous story in the Talmud (Hagigah 14b) of the four rabbis who entered the "orchard/

---

20. This idea is not compatible with Kurt Goedel's incompleteness theorem. See D. Hofstadter *Goedel, Escher, Bach: An Eternal Golden Braid.* Basic Books, 1979.

paradise," only one of whom (Rabbi Akiva) exited unscathed. Maimonides interprets this story as the rabbis engaging in Divine science and explains that only someone who has "achieved human perfection" (Pines, p. 68), as did Rabbi Akiva, can study and properly understand metaphysics. (Maimonides will have much more to say about human perfection in Book Three, chapter 27.) In chapter 33 Maimonides begins to explain his program for studying metaphysics, hinting at *the doctrine of negative attributes* (which he will discuss in depth in Book One, chapters 58 and 59) by saying that God "begins with . . . absolute negation" (Pines, p. 71) and stating that because of restrictions on promulgating certain ideas publicly (see above, chapter 17), only "flashes of [insight]" and "chapter headings (i.e., generalities, not specifics) may be transmitted" in the *Guide* to the "perfect[ed] man" (Pines, pp. 71–72).

Chapter 34 delineates five reasons why it is difficult to study philosophy and (thus) achieve perfection:

1. The material is difficult.

2. Not everyone is smart enough.

3. There are many prerequisites, "for whoever wishes to achieve human perfection . . . [must] train

44

himself . . . in . . . logic . . . , the mathematical sciences . . . , the natural sciences, and [only] after that in . . . divine science" (Pines, p. 75).

4. One needs the proper temperament. Maimonides points out that "moral virtues are a preparation for the rational virtues" (Pines, pp. 76–77), which again anticipates the argument Maimonides will make in Book Three (chapter 27) regarding the purpose of the commandments (to perfect the body so that one may then perfect his or her[21] soul). Maimonides cautions that the perfected individual is not overly emotional or passionate (e.g., easy to anger).

5. There are many distractions.

Chapter 34 also provides another way of comprehending God, besides negatively, by explaining that God cannot be "apprehend[ed] . . . except . . . [indirectly] through the things that He has made" (Pines, p. 74). In other words, one must use inductive rather than deductive logic in thinking about God (see Book One, chapter 54, where the concept of "attributes of action" is discussed).[22] In chapter 35, Maimonides

---

21. I will use the expression "his or her" as appropriate, although Maimonides, writing in the 12th century, assumed his readers were men.

22. Kaplan LJ, editor. *Maimonides – Between Philosophy and Halakhah:*

returns to the concept of God's incorporeality, and for the first time connects it with the notion of His absolute unity. Maimonides emphasizes the importance of this concept by saying that it "ought to be made clear and explained to everyone. . . ." (Pines, p. 81).

Chapters 36–45 are again lexicographic/definitional, and some of the terms discussed segue into the discussion of the "attributes" of God in chapters 51–60. Chapter 40 again discusses the concept of "divine intellectual overflow" (Pines, p. 90) first introduced above in chapter 2, which will be of supreme importance for Rambam's understanding of prophecy in Book Two (especially chapter 12). Chapter 41 discusses the equi-vocal term "soul" as it applies to man ("the remains of man after death" – Pines, p. 91) and to God ("[where] it has the meaning of will" – Pines. p. 91). This paves the way for Maimonides' explanation of life after death as the prepared soul uniting (in some way) with the Divine after death via the active intellect (see Book One, chapter 70). Chapter 43 further discusses angels, mentioning for the first time their incorporeality and some of the figurative

Rabbi Joseph B Soloveitchik's lectures on the Guide of the Perplexed. Ktav and Urim, Jerusalem and New York, 2016, pp. 102–4.

terms used by the Bible to describe them. Chapters 44 and 45 discuss the equi-vocal verbs "seeing" (again; see above chapter 28) and "hearing" as they apply to God. Chapter 46 is a long summary of Maimonides' notions about figurative terminology used in the Bible, in which he explains that the Bible was forced to use anthropomorphic terminology "in order that His acts should be [understood]" (Pines, p. 99). Chapters 47 and 48 return again to the discussion of "seeing" and "hearing" as they relate to God. Chapter 49 is another lexicographic/definitional chapter that again discusses the incorporeality of angels (see also chapter 43 above). Chapter 50 is a bridge – again discussing God's unity (see above, chapter 35) and leading into the discussion of the "attributes" of God in the following chapters.

Chapters 51–60 discuss the "attributes" of God. The word "attributes" is in quotes because according to Maimonides believing that God has attributes (e.g., that He is good, or wise) is like saying He has a body (Pines, p. 114 and 119). "God cannot be defined" (Pines, p. 115). God is also independent of time, place and motion (Pines, p. 117). In chapter 54 Maimonides explains that Moses asked to know God's "essence" and His "ways" (Exodus 33:13), and God replied that even he (Moses) would only be able to grasp how God governs the world – i.e., the "attributes of action" of God, but not His actual attributes (essence). Nevertheless, Moses, according to Maimonides, came the closest of anyone to "knowing" God (Pines, pp. 123–4). In other words, even Moses could only apprehend God indirectly (inductively, through knowledge of His actions) but not in any direct/deductive way.[23] Along these lines, Maimonides explains that when we say God is moral, we mean that He acts in ways "that in us proceed from moral qualities" (Pines, p. 124). When we say God is gracious, it is because "He . . . brings into existence and governs beings" (Pines, p. 125). "The purpose of all this is to show that the attributes ascribed to Him are attributes of His actions [,] . . . [not] that. . . . He possesses [positive attributes]" (Pines, p. 128).

So what can we say about God? According to Maimonides in chapters 58 and 59, we can basically say only negative things ("negations")[24] about Him

---

23. Kaplan, *ibid*. pp. 111 and 164–6.

24. The "doctrine of negative attributes" is based on Plotinus; see S Feldman, G*ersonides: Judaism Within the Limits of Reason*. Littman Library of Jewish Civilization. Oxford and Portland. 2010, p. 70. Similar discussions are found in the Islamic philosophical writings of Al-Farabi and Averroes;

(Pines, p. 134); as previously mentioned; this idea is referred to as *the doctrine of negative attributes*. For example, we can say God has no body, no emotions, no physical properties and is not subject to change. With every negative attribute "you come nearer to the apprehension of Him" (Pines, p. 138). The few "essential" affirmative attributes Maimonides allows about God (e.g., He exists, He is One) must be qualified by a negative (e.g., He exists, but His existence is not like any other [chapter 56]), and Maimonides insists that it be understood that these attributes are not distinct from God's essence (as our wisdom is from ourselves), but are *identical* with His essence. (The related ideas that God's intellect and knowledge are also identical with His essence will surface again in Book One, chapter 68 and in Book Three, chapter 20.) Furthermore, the only positive attributes we are allowed to utter about God are those that denote an action (e.g., that God created the universe),[25] but not an actual attribute (e.g., that God is good), unless the attribute is expressed in the Torah (which is

---

see S Feldman, *Levi Ben Gershom/Gersonides: The Wars of the Lord*, Volume two. Jewish Publication Society, Philadelphia, 1987, p. 6.

25. Feldman, *Gersonides*, p. 71.

written in the language of men; see the discussion above, in chapters 26 and 27) or if it was inserted into the prayer service by the Sages (the men of the Great Synagogue). Based on a verse in Psalms (65:2) Maimonides concludes that *silence* is the best way to praise God (Pines, p. 139). The best we can really hope to understand of the Divine order, according to Maimonides, is not to understand God Himself, but to comprehend the intervening intellects between God and man (see Book 2, chapters 4–12). Chapter 60 summarizes these ideas of God's "attributes," and concludes that "he who affirms that God . . . has positive attributes . . . has abolished his belief in the existence of . . . [God] without being aware of it" (Pines, p. 145), probably because positive attributes are limiting, and not compatible with God's ultimate simplicity and unity.[26]

Chapters 61–64 continue the discussion of God's "attributes" by discussing the significance of the Divine Names. As with the lexicographic/definitional chapters, most of the material in these chapters is self-explanatory. When Maimonides states "He is

---

26. Wolfson HA *Repercussions of the Kalam in Jewish Philosophy.* Harvard, 1979, p. 30.

existent not through existence" (Pines, p. 155) he is emphasizing that God's existence is different from that of everything else and that "[t]hese subtle notions . . . elude the mind. . . ." (Pines, p. 132), because our existence is tied to our bodies and motion/time, while God's is not (see also previously, chapters 52 and 57). In chapter 62 Maimonides explains that divine science (philosophy) is "the apprehension of the active intellect" (the lowest intelligence/emanation from God, the only one that can interact with humanity, indirectly; Pines, p. 152). At the end of chapter 64 Maimonides explains that the equi-vocal term "glory" can refer both to the praise of God and His essence.

Chapters 65–67 also continue the discussion of God's "attributes" and nearly conclude the lexico-graphic/definitional chapters of Book One. Chapters 65 and 67 discuss "speaking" or "saying" as they refer to God, connoting His will (Pines, p. 157), whilst chapter 66 tackles the verb "writing" (Pines, p. 160). Chapter 68 concludes the discussion of Divine "attributes" by discussing the Aristotelian notion that in the act of learning, the intellect and the object of knowledge become one. In the case of God, however, His essence *is* His intellect *and* His knowledge (and

His intellect and knowledge are not like any other); in addition He is the object and the subject of His own cognition. *Intellect* would then be another example of an equi-vocal noun, with different meanings when applied to God and man. (This idea will be discussed further in Book Three, chapter 20.) This Aristotelian notion that in the act of learning, the intellect and the object of knowledge become one, will help pave the way for Maimonides' explanation of life after death as the prepared human soul somehow becomes one with God (see Book One, chapter 70).

(2)

Chapters 69–76 for the most part are a polemic against the major branch of Islamic philosophy known as Kalam. Maimonides placed these chapters here, likely because he was dissatisfied with the Kalam's approach to explaining creation and God's incorporeality and unity, and he wished to present the inadequacies of their arguments before presenting his own arguments regarding creation at the beginning of Book Two. This final section of Book One requires a fair amount of background.

The word "Kalam" literally means "speech" or

"word" and is used in the sense of "scholastic theology";[27] theologians who are Kalam adherents are said to be "Mutakallimun" or masters of Kalam.[28] Sadia Gaon (10th century Babylonia), the first Rabbinic authority to write a book of philosophy,[29] which unlike the *Guide* was written to be plainly understood, was an adherent of some aspects of Kalam philosophy. While not mentioning Sadia by name, there are several instances where Rambam seems to be specifically targeting Sadia's thought (see below).

The somewhat repetitious Chapter 69 begins Maimonides' introduction to Kalam philosophy. In this chapter, Maimonides elaborates on the philosophical notion of God as First Cause or Prime Mover; this is the same argument used by Rambam to prove God's existence in the beginning of his Code of Jewish Law, the *Mishnah Torah* or *Yad Hachazakah* (*Hilchot Yesoday HaTorah* – Fundamentals of the Torah 1:5). Rambam asserts that the Kalam did not approve of the designation Prime Mover for the Deity because

---

27. M Fakhry, *A History of Islamic Philosophy*, third edition. Columbia, New York, 2004, p. xix.

28. Wolfson, *The Philosophy of the Kalam,* pp. 1–2.

29. S Rosenblatt, translator, *The Book of Beliefs and Opinions.* Yale University Press, New Haven and London, 1948, 1976.

according to their way of thinking, God being a Prime Mover implied that the world is eternal (see below); Maimonides will (in Book Two) give his proof of God's existence and unity, and his proof will specifically *not* depend upon whether or not the world was created in time or is eternal.

Rambam goes on to explain the four different Aristotelian "categories" of causality: the *formal* cause (the design, shape or form of an object), the *material* cause (the matter that the object is made of), the *final* cause (the final or end purpose of an object) and the *efficient* cause (what physically brought the object about). Thus, to use Wootton's example,[30] the four Aristotelian "causes" of a table are: its formal cause (its design), its final cause (providing a place on which to eat), its material cause (what it's made of) and its efficient cause (the tools used to fashion it). According to the Kalam, God as Maker is only the efficient cause of the world. According to Rambam, God is also the "form" and the final purpose ("end") of the world because His existence or "overflow" (more on this in Book Two, chapter 12) endows the world with its "permanence and constant existence" (Pines, p. 171).

---

30. Wootton, *op. cit.*, p. 69.

Chapter 70 is the only lexicographic/definitional chapter in this second section of Book One, and it discusses the figurative interpretation of a Biblical term (*rachav* – traveled; literally rode). In addition, this chapter includes further discussions of the soul and God as Prime Mover. Maimonides, continuing some thoughts from chapter 41, explains that the soul with which one is born is not the same as the soul with which one is left when he or she dies. The soul with which one is born is in a state of "preparedness" or potentiality (Pines, p. 174); at the time of one's death one's soul represents all that one has accomplished in life in apprehending God to the limit of human abilities, and it is only the soul that is sufficiently accomplished in this regard that can somehow unite with an aspect of the Divine after death via the active intellect. Immortality for Maimonides, then, "is not a promise, but a task."[31]

Chapter 71 presents Maimonides' understanding of Kalam philosophy.[32] In the second paragraph of this chapter, Maimonides mentions "some *geonim* [the leaders of the academies in Babylonia and Israel fol-

---

31. Kaplan, *op. cit.*, p. 159.

32. Wolfson, *op. cit.*, pp. 43–58, 84, and 175–184.

lowing the time of the Talmud]" (Pines, p. 176) whose ideas about the unity of God are similar to those of the Mutakalimun. Maimonides here is referring to Sadia Gaon, but (politely?) not mentioning him by name.[33] He then mentions the two main branches of Kalam philosophy, the Mutazilites and the Asharites. In brief, the *Mutazilites*, who arose first, were (as was Maimonides) against the notion of God's corporeality, divested God of positive attributes and believed in free will. Theologically they focused on the notion of Divine justice and the rationality of God's ways, and thus argued that God cannot "do" what is contrary to reason (e.g., to proclaim that 2 + 2 = 5) nor could He act with total disregard for the welfare of His creations.[34] The *Asharites*, on the other hand, felt that the latter arguments, as well as allowing for humanity's free will, implied limits, and were thus affronts to God's power. In addition, based on verses in the Koran that they were unwilling to interpret figuratively, they argued that God did have positive attributes.[35] Finally, they believed that matter was formed of atoms (Pines,

33. HA Davidson, *Maimonides the Rationalist*. Oxford and Portland, 2011, p. 170.

34. Fakhry, *op. cit.*, pp. 44–56.

35. Fakhry, *op. cit.*, pp. 215–23.

p. 178), and the idea of the randomness of atoms was linked with their denial of causality.[36] It is with the Mutalizite branch of Kalam that Sadia Gaon seemed mainly to identify, but some of his arguments were reminiscent of those of Asharites as well (see the discussion in chapters 74–76 of Book One).

Maimonides then begins to present what he believes are weaknesses with Kalam philosophy. First he says, "they follow the imagination and . . . [not their] intellect" (Pines, p. 179); Maimonides will have more to say about this in the last part of chapter 73 of Book One. Second, they base their proof of God's existence on the world's being created in time. Because Maimonides believes that "with regard to . . . the eternity of the world or its temporal creation – no cogent demonstration can be reached" (Pines, p. 180), as already mentioned, he will not take this approach. Maimonides then outlines his method for proving

---

36. Wolfson, *op. cit.*, pp. 468–71. Lucretius, the Greek philosopher who first posited the existence of atoms, believed that the universe was the result of the random interaction of these atoms, and thus he believed there was no cause and effect. It seems to me that one could believe in atoms *and* causality although this did not appear to be intellectually appealing to ancient or medieval followers of Lucretius. See Wootton, *op. cit.*, p. 8, footnote v. Maimonides also believed that some Kalam ideas were derived from the Church. See Wolfson, *op. cit.*, pp. 48–56.

God's existence, which again does not depend upon whether or not the world was created in time: If the world was created in time, then it must have a Creator who created it in time. If not, then there still must be a Prime Mover, Who initiated motion and maintains that motion (Pines, pp. 181–2 and 243–6).

Maimonides then lays out the plan for the next several chapters of the *Guide*. He will discuss the premises of Kalam philosophy in chapter 73. In chapters 74–76 he will refute various Kalam proofs for the creation of the world in time and out of nothing (*ex nihilo*), for the unity of God and against the corporality of God. He will then delineate the premises and methodology of those he considers true philosophers in Book 2, chapters 1–12, followed by his discussion of creation.

Chapter 72 does not seem to play a critical role in Maimonides' plan for this second section of Book One, because Maimonides does not describe its contents in advance. In this long chapter, Maimonides discusses the universe as he understood it. In medieval cosmology each planet (which included the moon, the sun and the five planets visible to the naked eye) moved within a sphere or spheres surrounding the Earth, which was in the center. Because of their movement, the sun, moon, planets and stars were thought to be animate, with a soul and desire (at least for knowledge), and were identified with angels (Divine messengers). Above the spheres were separate intelligences, above whom was God.[37] In this chapter Maimonides also acknowledges the paradox of God being both "separate from the world" while at the same time, governing it (Pines, pp. 192–3), albeit indirectly (see below).

Chapter 73 begins Maimonides' critique of Kalam philosophy, mainly its Asharite branch. In this chapter he discusses twelve Kalam philosophical premises, some of which connect to their philosophical arguments, and which will be discussed by Maimonides in the coming three chapters. Maimonides will refute some of these premises individually or in combination in the following chapters of Book One.

The first premise of Kalam philosophy is that of atoms, which, as we have already mentioned, is a premise mainly of the Asharite branch of the Kalam. The second and third premises are consequences of belief in atoms. The fourth and fifth premises discuss *accidents*, or nonessential characteristics of matter/atoms. The sixth premise is the lack of cause and ef-

37. Goodman, *op. cit.,* pp. 213–4.

fect, which again, is a premise mainly of the Asharite branch of Kalam philosophy. This premise necessitates God's continuing acts of creation in order to sustain the world/universe. As Maimonides illustrates towards the end of this section, some Mutakallimun are so extreme in their denial of cause and effect that they believe that when pen is put to paper, writing occurs not because ink flows from the pen to the paper, but because God continually wills the paper to turn black when the tip of the pen touches the paper. (I have combined two different examples here from Pines, p. 202). According to these Mutakallimun even human free will requires continual Divine action. Man is not even free to perform religious acts; this extreme idea, of course, has important implications vis-à-vis reward and punishment and is a large part of the reason Maimonides and others rejected this Kalam approach. Maimonides ends his discussion of the sixth premise with a mocking tone. (The Kalam idea of the absence of cause and effect will surface again in Book Three, chapter 17, the "third opinion.") The next three premises again relate to the Kalam ideas of atoms and accidents (non-essential characteristics).

Premises ten, eleven and twelve of Kalam philosophy as presented by Maimonides are the ones he will take the most pains to refute in the following chapter. The tenth premise relates to the Kalam inability to distinguish between imagination and reason. (This is related to Premise twelve as well.) This is because the Kalam believe the notion that anything "that may be imagined is an admissible notion for the intellect" (Pines, p. 206). Maimonides does concede that the Mutakalimun agree that two opposite statements "cannot be admitted by the intellect" (Pines, p. 207); however, he argues against Kalam premise ten by posing a counter-example: "something the imagination considers as necessary [but which] is impossible – namely, that God . . . [has] . . . a body" (Pines, p. 211). Maimonides will provide further arguments against the tenth premise in the following chapter.[38]

Premise eleven of the Kalam is that infinity is im-

---

38. Despite its importance for prophecy (see below and Book Two), Maimonides was not all that enamored by imagination (or the imaginative faculty, as he called it) because he thought it could (unlike the intellect) lead to absurd thoughts. A famous example brought by Maimonides is that of a chariot of iron that could fly through the air (See his introduction to the Chapters of the Father's, part of Maimonides commentary on the Mishnah, also known, descriptively, as the Eight Chapters, translated in RL Weiss and C Butterworth, *Ethical Writings of Maimonides.* New York University 1975, Dover reprint 1983, p. 63). While it may be too much to expect Maimonides to have been able to envision an airplane, he was obviously unduly harsh in his critique of flights of fancy (pun intended).

possible. Maimonides refutes this claim in chapter 73 of Book One by bringing Aristotelian arguments that, at least potentially, even in the real world infinities are possible, such as divisions of time, and that "no absurdity will follow . . . [the] affirmation of the possibility of an infinite . . . succession[,] and that no demonstration has been advanced against its possibility."[39] Here, Maimonides follows Aristotle, who distinguished between *actual* infinity, which Aristotle thought impossible, and *potential* infinity. The lack of actual infinity meant for Aristotle, for example, that the universe could not be infinitely large. However, Aristotle realized that counting has no end, that time or a given length can be divided into infinitely smaller portions, and that cyclical events with a finite number of possibilities can go on forever (e.g., sunrise-sunset). This Aristotelian idea of potential infinity will be crucial for Maimonides' refutation of several Kalam arguments in the next chapter.

Premise twelve is that the Kalam do not always trust their senses (this is related to Premise ten, because many things that can be imagined may never be

---

39. Wolfson, *op. cit.*, p. 433. In modern mathematics, there are many orders of infinity.

sensed because they do not exist, e.g., a unicorn; but see footnote 38). Maimonides will refute this premise as well in the following chapter.

In chapter 74 Maimonides examines the Kalam proofs for the creation of the world in time and *ex nihilo* (out of nothing). Along the way he will connect these arguments with different Kalam philosophical premises and disprove them. The first Kalam proof for the creation of the world in time (i.e., creation after a period of non-existence) analogizes from the world as it is.[40] Since we see things develop in the world (e.g. people from semen, trees from seeds), the world requires an "artificer" or builder (Pines, p. 215). However, Maimonides contends, this argument proves only that there is a Creator, not that He created the world in time, out of nothing.[41] The second Kalam proof for the creation of the world in time takes this argument a step further, by adding that since infinity is impossible according to Kalam premise eleven (last chapter), then the Earth had to be created from nothing (*ex nihilo*) at some time in the past. However, as we have already mentioned, because of the Aristotelian argument

---

40. Wolfson, *op. cit.*, pp. 382–5.

41. Wolfson, *op. cit.*, p. 384; Efodi, *Sefer Moreh Nevuchim*, Part I, p. 125, note 2.

that potentially infinite sequences do exist (e.g., the developmental cycle of seed-individual-seed-individual is just the sort of infinity that Aristotle thought possible), Maimonides could argue that this second Kalam proof is based on a false premise, and again only proves there is a Creator, not that He created the world in time.

The third Kalam proof for the creation of the world in time is similar to the first, and relates to the aggregation and segregation of atoms;[42] this is also a proof brought by Sadia Gaon,[43] although Sadia does not use the term atoms. This proof argues that the substances of the world can either "be aggregated or separated . . . [and therefore they] require someone who aggregates . . . and separates" (Pines, p. 216). Again, this argument proves only that there is a Creator (Aggregator and Separator), not that He created, aggregated or segregated the world in time, out of nothing.[44]

The fourth Kalam proof takes the third one a step further, and also tries to show that the world was cre-

---

42. Wolfson, *op. cit.*, pp. 386–92.

43. Rosenblatt, *op. cit.*, pp. 42–43. The second Kalam proof (above) is also brought by Sadia Gaon, *ibid.* p. 44.

44. Wolfson, *op. cit.*, p. 388; Efodi, *Sefer Moreh Nevuchim*, Part I, p. 126, note 4.

ated in time, by adding that the aggregation and separation of atoms cannot have gone on forever, because infinity is impossible according to Kalam premise eleven. Sadia implicitly used this argument as well.[45] Maimonides again is able to reject this Kalam proof for creation of the world in time using the Aristotelian argument that potentially infinite sequences (such as cycles of aggregation – separation) do indeed exist.

The fifth Kalam proof for the creation of the world in time relates to the notion of *particularization*:[46] Since everything in the sublunar world is particularized (in terms of shape and size, for example), there must exist a Particularizer who particularized the world. (See also Book One, chapter 17.) Similarly, the sixth Kalam proof for the creation of the world in time is an argument from *preponderation*.[47] Again, a similar theme: Because the world exists, there is a preponderance (predominance) of existence to nonexistence. Therefore *someone* had to cause this preponderance of existence. However, both of these proofs fail because the reasoning is circular; the premise (that

---

45. Rosenblatt, *op. cit.,* p. 42; see also Wolfson, *op. cit.,* p. 425.

46. Wolfson, *op. cit.,* pp. 434–444.

47. Wolfson, *op. cit.,* pp. 449–52.

the world exists for proof six or that everything is particularized in proof five) is the very thing that is sought to be proven! (See also chapter 76, below, third proof.) Maimonides could also argue here, as he did previously vis-à-vis aggregation and separation, that just because there is a Particularizer or a Preponderator, that does not mean that the particularization or the preponderation occurred in time. Maimonides could have also used the circular reasoning argument earlier. Perhaps Maimonides was really showing two ways to argue against each of these Kalam proofs.

The seventh and final Kalam proof for the creation of the world in time discussed by Maimonides in chapter 74 is an argument from the immortality of the intellect/soul,[48] and again makes use of the eleventh Kalam premise that infinity is impossible. The argument is that if the world is eternal, there must have been an infinite number of men who died in the past and also an infinite number of souls, which according to Kalam premise eleven is impossible. Therefore the world must have been created in time. This argument would seem to be harder for Maimonides to refute, because here we are dealing not with a potential infin-

---

48. Wolfson, *op. cit.*, pp. 452–5.

ity but with an actual infinity (the number of souls). Nevertheless, Maimonides argues that since the soul unites in some way with the Divine/active intellect after death (this idea was common also among Moslem philosophers of the time),[49] there are never actually an infinite number of independent souls "around" at any given time, so there is no clear-cut Kalam proof for creation of the world in time.

Chapter 75 discusses five Kalam proofs for the unity of God. The first is the "method of mutual hindering."[50] If there were more than one deity, each deity could cause a contrary to take place (e.g., one wishes the weather to be warm, the other for it to be cold), which is impossible. Thus, the Deity must be One. This argument is also brought by Sadia Gaon.[51] Maimonides argues against this by showing that it would be possible to have one deity in the sublunar world and one in the heavens; in this way there would

49. See Pines, p. 221, (footnotes 10 and 11). See also Fakhry, *op. cit.*, p. 301; JL Kraemer, *Maimonides: The Life and World of One of Civilization's Greatest Mind.* Doubleday. 2008, p. 584 note 46; Davidson, *Rationalist*, p. 184; Wolfson, *op. cit.*, pp. 452–5; S Feldman, *Levi Ben Gershom/Gersonides*: *The Wars of the Lord*, Volume one. Jewish Publication Society, Philadelphia, 1984, p. 40, footnote 21.

50. Wolfson, *op. cit.*, pp. 49 and 56.

51. Rosenblatt, *op. cit.*, p. 98.

be no hindrance of one with the other because they rule in separate realms. Furthermore, Maimonides argues, this does not limit the power of one deity or the other because "it [is not] a deficiency for an artificer to have no power over what is impossible for him" (Pines, p. 224), just as it is impossible for God to declare $2 + 2 = 5$.

The second Kalam proof for the unity of God relies on differentiating gods, one from the other. For example, if there were more than one deity, different notions would apply to each one (otherwise they wouldn't be different), which appears again to limit each deity in some way. However, Maimonides counters this argument by reminding us that one god can also have multiple "[negative] attributes" so that "it would not be impossible that either of the two gods should possess several [negative] notions, some of which he would have in common with the other god, while differing from the latter through the possession of others" (Pines, p. 224). Presumably, because it wasn't positive attributes distinguishing one god from another, there could be nothing "positively" different about them.

The third Kalam proof for the unity of God relies on the notion of will, and that there can only be one will of God. However, using similar reasoning to that used in the method of "mutual hindrance," why couldn't there be more than one will if there were more than one god active at once in different realms, e.g., one in the sublunar world, and one in the heavens?

The fourth Kalam proof for the unity of God is that if there existed more than one god, there is no difference if we assume two or more gods. However, this in and of itself does not prove that God is one, for, as Maimonides argues: "Just as the Christians think that He is three, and it is not so, we think that He is one [using these arguments of the Mutakalimun], [but] the matter [may] not [be] so" (Pines, p, 225).

The fifth Kalam argument for the unity of God is "the argument from need."[52] If one deity can create the universe, then the other is not necessary, and if both deities are needed then there seems to be a limitation in at least one of them. However, Maimonides refutes the last claim by arguing, similarly as he did the first argument of this chapter, that just as it is no limitation of God that He cannot turn Himself into a body, the fact that one deity could not create on his own would not necessarily be a limitation. (This

---

52. Wolfson, *op. cit.*, p. 49.

counter-argument seems weak to me, because God turning Himself into a body may be logically impossible, unlike the situation of God not being able to create on His own.)

Book One ends with chapter 76, which discusses three Kalam proofs against the corporeality of God. The first proof is that God might actually have a body like no other body. (This is not too dissimilar from Rambam's refutation of the notion that God had a body, although one "more resplendent than . . . themselves, and . . . composed . . . not [of] flesh and blood" [Pines, p. 21]). The Kalam try to dismiss this argument using their premises one and five (see above, chapter 73). Rambam dismisses this argument as a self-contradiction.[53]

The second Kalam argument against corporeality is similar to the first, but a bit more sophisticated. Here the argument is that God has a "body," but that "body" is an equi-vocal term, and means something completely different (e.g., "perfect" or" noble essence" – Pines, p. 229) when applied to God. Sadia too makes a similar claim.[54] However, like the first argument,

---

53. Wolfson, *op. cit.*, p. 77.

54. Rosenblatt, *op. cit.*, p. 96.

this more sophisticated argument is also essentially a self-contradiction as well as a positive attribute, which later Mutakalimun recognized as well.[55]

The third and similar Kalam proof for God's incorporeality reduces the contrary argument to an absurdity, to wit: If the deity had a body, it would be finite and have certain characteristics (e.g., shape and size). But if that is the case, someone would have had to particularize the Deity, i.e., decide what size and shape He should be, and this is not possible. Maimonides claims that this proof is based on the premise of particularization (see the fifth Kalam proof for the creation of the world, in chapter 74, above) and that the reasoning is (again) circular ("would lead to an infinite series;" Pines, p.230).

---

55. Wolfson, *op. cit.*, pp. 14–15.

Introduction to Book Two

NOW THAT MAIMONIDES HAS SHOWN THE deficiency of the Kalam's approach regarding the existence of God and creation, His incorporeality and His unity, he will proceed with his own philosophical approach. As he did when he began his discussion of Kalam philosophy, Maimonides begins with (25 Aristotelian) philosophical premises.

The first three premises deal with actual (as opposed to potential) infinity, that Maimonides agrees is impossible (see the discussion of infinity in Book One, chapter 73, premise 11). The next dozen premises are self-explanatory. In premise sixteen, "multiplicity cannot be cognized" if something is not a body (i.e., matter), because only matter allows for individuation/particularization; in other words, there can be multiple chairs but only one idea or ideal of a chair. Maimonides will use this premise in Book Two, chapter 1 to help prove God's unity.

In premises nineteen and twenty Maimonides distinguishes between things that exist due to a cause (premise nineteen) and things that exist without a cause. Things that exist due to a cause are only potentially (or contingently) existent (because without the cause they would not exist); thus there must also exist at least one cause whose very existence is essential (premise twenty).[56] Premise twenty and the notion of a prime (or proximate) mover (premise twenty-five) will form the bases of Maimonides' proof of God's existence in chapters 1 and 2 of Book Two. Maimonides adds a twenty-sixth "hypothesis" that "time and movement are eternal, perpetual" and reminds us that heavens and their movements are "not subject to generation and corruption" (Pines, p. 240). Premises 21–24 basically postulate that everything has two "essential" properties (matter and form), as well as non-essential characteristics, referred to as "accidents," such as quantity, shape and position.

---

56. J Gutmann. Maimonides, *The Guide of the Perplexed. Abridged, with Introduction and Commentary*. Hackett, Indianapolis, 1995, p. 213.

Book Two

(1)

The first two chapters of Book Two use the Proximate/Prime/First Mover argument to prove God's existence. Maimonides does this in chapter 1, using many of the premises he listed in the Introduction to Book Two. He then argues for the Unity of God in several ways, using different arguments than those of the Mutakallimun presented at the end of Book One. First, Maimonides argues that since God is not a force or (a force in a) body (Pines, pp. 249–50), He cannot be individuated into more than one being (recall premise sixteen of the Introduction to Book Two). Second, he argues that if there were more than one deity, neither of them can then be the first cause. Third, if there were two (or more) deities, they would need to cooperate in some way (e.g., to agree to operate in separate realms, such as supralunar vs lunar), and this act of cooperation would require an agent to cause it to happen, which would make that (single) agent the Deity. (Presumably it is this last argument which Maimonides feels makes his proof for God's unity better than the first Kalam proof brought in Book One, chapter 75.)

In chapters 1 and 2 Maimonides again (see Book One, chapter 17) makes use of the Ptolemaic astronomical system, in which all of the five visible planets, the moon, the sun and the stars were assumed (incorrectly, of course) to orbit the Earth. Maimonides, following Ptolemy and Aristotle, divides the universe into sublunar and lunar areas. The sublunar area, where we reside, consists of the four Greek "elements:" Earth, water, air and fire.[57] The moon, sun, planets and stars reside in the supralunar realm in different spheres (see also Book Two, chapter 10) that surround the Earth. Because the spheres move, they were thought to be intelligent and possess a soul; thus, they were also referred to as intelligences and according to Maimonides, correspond to the Biblical concept of angels. Each sphere was thought to have an effect upon and make contact with the sphere below it, like the layers of an onion, because a vacuum was thought to represent a

---

57. Wootton, *op. cit.*, p. 112. See also *Mishnah Torah, Hilchot Yesoday ha-Torah,* Fundamentals of the Torah, chapter 3 and the previous discussion in Book One, chapter 17.

logical contradiction (the existence of nonexistence).[58]
Maimonides again emphasizes "the existence of the
deity . . . that has no cause . . . is proved by cogent
and certain demonstrations, regardless of whether the
world has come into being in time after having been
nonexistent . . . or . . . not" (Pines, p. 252).

In chapters 3–12, Maimonides further discusses
medieval physics as a background to his discussions
of creation, prophecy, divine science (*maaseh merkavah*) and God's knowledge in the rest of Book Two.
In chapters 4 and 5 Maimonides reiterates (e.g., from
the previous chapter, Pines, p. 253) the medieval
position that the spheres have souls and intellects
(or intelligences, as they are often referred to), are
rational (as evidenced by their motion) and correspond to angels ("the intellects are the angels," Pines,
p. 250; "Aristotle . . . speaks of . . . intellects, and
we speak of angels," Pines, p. 262). He also discusses
the notion of the *active intellect*, which is based on
the notion that there are nine immaterial intellects,

---

58. Goodman, *op. cit*, p. 262. See also NH Strickman "Abraham ibn Ezra: On
seeing God's back," Hakirah 2017; 23: 113–34, esp. pp. 123–6. I have presented
only an overview of medieval astronomy for simplicity, and because the
primary and secondary sources seem to differ in many of the specifics. See
the references in this and the previous footnote, for example.

or levels, separating God from man. God is above it all, and in this philosophical worldview, "does not do things in a direct fashion" (Pines, p. 258). Rather, He "brought into existence the first intellect, who is the mover of the first sphere" (Pines, p. 258). God, being omniscient, was also imagined to be overflowing with knowledge, which emanates from Him to the first intellect until it finally reaches the lowest of the intellects corresponding to the moon, just above the Earth. At that level, there occurs the final heavenly emanation that reaches us in the sublunar world; this is the *active intellect* – the lowest level of Godly intelligence – to which the perfected man has potential access. The active intellect is able to interact with us (who are composed of the four elements) in the sublunar world, allowing us to perceive the world around us and have a grasp of the Divine. God acts *directly* at most only with the first intellect, and thus interacts *indirectly* with everything else ("God . . . does not do things in a direct form" – Pines, p. 258).

Chapters 6 and 7 are again lexicographic/definitional chapters, discussing the term "angel" as it relates to the concepts Maimonides introduced in the two preceding chapters. Here again Maimonides will use definitions to further his philosophical agenda.

For example, Maimonides states that "every form in which an angel is seen, exists in the vision of prophecy" and "every vision of an angel occurs only in a vision of prophecy" (Pines, p. 265). Therefore, the incident of Balaam and the talking she-ass (see also Book Two, chapter 42) was all a vision, according to Maimonides;[59] cf. Book Three, chapter 24. Another similar point Maimonides makes here is "that the intellect is [also] called a cherub" (Pines, pp. 264–5); this idea will be followed up in Book Two, chapters 12 and 45 as well as Book Three, chapter 45.[60]

Chapters 8–11 discuss philosophical matters of concern mainly for medieval cosmology. For example, chapter 8 discusses the question of whether the motion of the spheres generates sound. Interestingly,

---

59. If every encounter with an angel is a vision, one can also interpret the binding of Isaac as a vision (Gen. 22:11–12), removing the entire problem of how God could ask Abraham to sacrifice his son; it was a vision all along, i.e., Abraham is imagining what he would do if God were to ask him to sacrifice his beloved Isaac. When Abraham awakens from his vision or trance, he realizes the depth of his commitment to God. I am indebted to my brother, Rabbi Jeffrey (Shalom) Katz, for this insight. As shown by Shapiro, *Changing the Immutable*, pp. 67–73, Efodi (Profiat Duran ca. 1350–ca. 1415) in uncensored texts, clearly stated that Maimonides felt that the binding of Isaac was a vision or dream.

60. I am indebted to Baruch Shwartz for this insight (see http://thetorah.com/does-god-speak/, accessed 8/8/20).

even though the Bible seems to state that it does (Ezekiel 1:24–25), because philosophers "proved" that it didn't, Maimonides sides with the philosophers ("the conclusion whose demonstration is correct is believed" – Pines, p. 267), with some support from the Talmud (*Pesachim* 94b), where, in certain instances, the position of the wise men of the world is acknowledged to be correct and that of the rabbis, incorrect. Chapters 9 and 11 discuss questions of medieval astronomy (e.g., whether Venus and Mars are above or below the sun, relative to the Earth, which is at the center of the universe in medieval cosmology). Chapter 10 again discusses the four elements. Chapter 11 leads into another discussion of Divine overflow.

Chapter 12 delves into the concept of Divine Overflow in more detail. "[T]he world derives from the overflow of God . . . He has caused to overflow to it everything in it that is produced in time. . . . In the same way . . . He caused His knowledge to overflow to the prophets. His [indirect] action . . . is called overflow" (Pines, p. 279). Along the way, Maimonides justifies his position with verses from the Bible. For example, the verse "In thy light do we see light" (Psalm 36:10) is said to represent "the overflow of the intellect that has overflowed from Thee . . . [allowing us to] intellectually cognize" (Pines, p. 280).

(2)

The next major section of Book Two, chapters 13–31, discusses creation. Along the way, Maimonides will point out (mainly in chapters 15–24) shortcomings in Aristotle's approach (generally related to Aristotle's idea of an eternal universe), while the last two chapters (30 and 31) are lexicographic/definitional. In this section, we will note what appears to be a contradiction in how Maimonides explains various philosophical positions regarding creation, and the contradiction's implication, assuming the contradiction was intentional on Maimonides' part. (Recall the discussion of contradictions in Maimonides' Introduction to the *Guide*).

In chapter 13 Maimonides introduces the topic of creation. He explains that there are four opinions regarding creation: The first opinion, which Maimonides ascribes to Moses (and Abraham), is that there is an eternal God who created the world out of nothing (*ex nihilo*). A second opinion is ascribed to Plato: that there is an eternal God as well as "[eternal] matter that is eternal as the Deity is eternal. . . . They do not believe that it has the same rank in what exists as He. . . . He is the cause of its existence . . . and that He creates in it (or from it, i.e., the eternal matter) whatever He wishes." Maimonides identifies the third opinion with Aristotle, who believed in an eternal God and in eternal matter that "has never ceased to be and will never do so" (Pines, p. 284). The final opinion is that of Epicurus, that there is no God (and therefore no Divine Providence); Maimonides dismisses the latter opinion because "the existence of the Deity has already been demonstrated [as the First Cause or Prime Mover]" (Pines, p. 285). Maimonides concludes by saying that: "the purpose of every follower of the law of Moses and Abraham . . . is to believe that there is nothing eternal in any way existing simultaneously with God . . . [and that] the bringing into existence of a being out of nonexistence is for the Deity not an impossibility. . . ." (Pines, p. 285). In other words, any follower of Moses cannot believe in Plato's or Aristotle's ideas of creation because they both involve belief in something that existed alongside God, and that *ex-nihilo* creation is not impossible (otherwise even God couldn't do it, as even He can't make 2 + 2 = 5).

In chapters 14 through 24 Maimonides points out

shortcomings in Aristotle's approach, which assumes that both God and matter are eternal. Chapter 14 starts by listing Aristotle's reasons to believe the world is eternal, which Maimonides will then refute in chapters 15–21.

The first four Aristotelian arguments that Maimonides cites for the eternity of the world rely on at least one of two medieval philosophical notions: that circular motion does not decay and that heavenly matter is different from earthly matter in that heavenly matter also does not decay (see the discussion in Book One, chapter 17).[61]

The last three Aristotelian arguments for the eternity of the world (matter) in chapter 14 are related to the following idea: If the world was created in time, that implies that God changed in some way (or at least changed a certain potentiality of His to an actuality, or changed His mind, because before creation there was nothing; after creation – matter existed!), and any change in God is problematic, because He can't be perfect in two different situations: either He was perfect before the universe existed, or He became

---

61. For more details, see Goodman, *Maimonides*, pp. 174–6.

perfect after. These arguments will be refuted below, in Book Two, chapter 18.

In chapters 15 and 16 Maimonides reiterates his position that Aristotle had no proof ("demonstration" – Pines, p. 289) for the eternity of the world. This implies a certain "philosophical modesty" and allows for some truths to be revealed only through prophesied revelation.[62] In chapter 17 Maimonides argues that we are limited in understanding what may have occurred before creation ("pre-eternity" in chapter 14),[63] and uses this idea to argue against Aristotle who utilized proofs from the world as it is *now* to demonstrate that the universe is eternal. Imagine, Maimonides writes in the *Parable of the Island*, that a boy and his father were stranded on a desert island and the boy had never seen a woman. If the father would tell the boy about his mother, about how the boy developed within her womb and how she suckled him as a baby, the son would have no frame of reference for believing his father! As Maimonides puts it "a being's state of . . . completion, furnishes no indication of the state of that

---

62. Feldman, *Gersonides*, pp. 200–1.

63. This is similar today to the situation of physicists who cannot say what preceded the Big Bang.

being ['s] preceding. . . ." (Pines, pp. 297–8). In other words, we cannot (unlike what Aristotle attempted) "infer any reliable information about how an object came into being from what we observe about the object (as it currently exists)."[64] Again, Maimonides repeats: "we do not wish to establish as true that the world is created in time . . . what we wish to establish is the *possibility* [my emphasis] of its being created in time" (Pines, p. 298).

Chapter 18 again emphasizes how little we can understand about God, such as "His wisdom in making it necessary that the spheres [i.e., intelligences] should be nine" (Pines, p. 301). "The universe is consequent upon His perpetual and immutable wisdom. But we are completely ignorant of the rule of that wisdom and of the decision[s] made by it." (Pines, p. 302). Similarly, God's will is unlike human will because God has no impediments, except those that He Himself imposed (e.g., not to act against the universe as He created it, such as not allowing 2 + 2 to equal 5). God can also will something without there being any change in Him. Note how this argument refutes the last three Aristotelian arguments for the eternity of

64. Goodman, *op. cit.*, p. 225.

the world in Book Two, chapter 14, above. Furthermore, God's will is evident in otherwise inexplicable "facts" of nature. The example used by Maimonides is that there are nine heavenly spheres or intelligences, (and not eight or fifteen); a modern example could be why there are three laws of motion, or why there are "laws" of nature at all.[65] Perhaps because God's will has no impediments, one might be able to argue that God can create matter out of nothing. (See also the following paragraph.)

In chapter 19 Maimonides makes a different argument for proof of God's *will* in the universe. Maimonides takes it as proven that God exists (see Book Two, chapters 1 and 2). He then argues that because stars are fixed while planets move, that stars and planets are each composed of different types of matter;[66] i.e., they have been particularized (distinguished). Thus there must be a Particularizer. Maimonides recognizes that this is similar to a previous Kalam argument (Book One, chapter 74, fifth proof), but he believes the Kalam argument more trivial, since their evidence from

---

65. Wootton, *op. cit.,* chapter 9.

66. It has already been pointed out that this is not assumed to be true in modern physics.

particularization was based on trivial characteristics such as shape and size, not on "philosophical premises derived from the nature of that which exists" (Pines, p. 304). Once there is a Particularizer, and He exercised His will to particularize two different kinds of matter, He can also exercise His will to create matter out of nothing if He so desired, or to perform miracles. *This is Maimonides' main contribution to Jewish philosophy – taking the God of the philosophers (i.e., Aristotle) and showing that He can exercise His will and act as the God of Scripture.* (See further on this idea in Book Two, chapter 25.) Chapter 20 summarizes these arguments. Chapter 21 repeats Maimonides' stated "preference in favor of the world's having been produced in time" (Pines, p. 317), and argues against the concept that the world emanated from God, but rather that "the world has come about through an act of the Deity or through his particularization" (Pines, p. 315).

In chapter 22 Maimonides concludes that "[e]verything that Aristotle has said about all that exists from beneath the sphere of the moon to the center of the earth is indubitably correct. . . . On the other hand, everything upon which Aristotle expounds, with regard to the sphere of the moon and that which is above it, is . . . analogous to guessing" (Pines, pp. 319–20). Chapters 23 and 24 emphasize this point again and rationalize it by explaining that "in his [Aristotle's] time mathematics had not yet been brought to perfection!" (Emphasis mine, Pines, p. 326; see also Pines, p. 308). Chapter 24 discusses an idea that was important for medieval Ptolemaic cosmology – that of epicycles, and mentions Ptolemy's astronomy textbook, the *Almagest*.[67]

Chapter 25 is a key chapter of the *Guide*. The chapter begins with an oft-quoted comment of Maimonides: "Know that our shunning the affirmation of the eternity of the world is not due to a text . . . in the Torah. . . . For the texts indicating that the world has been produced in time are not more numerous than those indicating that the deity is a body. Nor are the gates of figurative interpretation shut in our faces. . . ." (Pines, p. 327). This incredibly bold statement of Maimonides is one reason so many people care what Maimonides said in the twelfth century, even though twelfth century cosmology has been completely overturned. To take just the most obvious examples, it allows us to "figuratively" understand

Genesis 1 while acknowledging the scientific truths of physics, evolution and genetics. How bold Rambam's approach truly is can be gauged by the opposition to allegorical interpretation of the Torah by other towering medieval figures such as the Rashbah (Solomon ben Abraham Aderet, ca. 1235–ca. 1310).[68] Allegorization of the Torah allows Maimonides to accept "the conclusion whose demonstration is correct" (Pines, p. 267) even if that conclusion appears to "contradict" the (literal meaning of the) Torah.

Maimonides continues: The problem with "the belief in eternity the way Aristotle sees it . . . that no nature changes at all, and that the customary course of events cannot be modified . . . destroys the Law in its principle . . . gives the lie to every miracle, and reduces to inanity all the hopes and threats that the law held out, unless . . . one interprets the miracles figuratively also. . . . If, however, one believed in eternity accord-

68. See for example, *Encyclopedia Judaica*, 1st ed. Keter, Jerusalem, 1974, volume 2, column 306 and G Stern, "Allegories of Torah and the story of their persecution in Languedoc (1305)," TheTorah.com, accessed 11/11/15. Some have argued that this strongly worded pro-allegorical interpretation argument of Maimonides is in direct response to the comments of the Rabad (see footnote 10) regarding those who were misled by *literal* interpretations of various Biblical verses into thinking that God had a body (Rabbi Moshe Soloveitchik, personal communication 2/20/17).

ing to . . . Plato – according to which the heavens . . . *are* [emphasis mine] subject to [change] this . . . would *not* [emphasis mine] destroy the foundations of the law and would be followed not by the lie being given to miracles, but by their becoming admissible [because God could then exert His will in the heavens]. . . . However, no necessity could impel us to do this unless this opinion were demonstrated" (Pines, pp. 328–9). This is an important point. Maimonides does not believe that there is a demonstration (i.e., proof) that Aristotle is correct about the eternity of the universe, but if Aristotle were correct, there would be no concept of miracles. Maimonides then concludes, as might be expected: "Know that with belief in the creation of the world out of nothing, all the miracles become possible" (Pines, p. 329). However, is this really Maimonides' position?

As pointed out by Herbert Davidson,[69] here in chapter 25 Maimonides argues that while Aristotle's

---

69. H Davidson, "Maimonides' Secret Position on Creation" in I. Twersky, *Studies in Medieval Jewish History and Literature*. Harvard, Cambridge, MA and London, 1979, pp. 16–38. Oddly, despite a forceful presentation found convincing by me as well as many scholars (e.g., M Shapiro, personal communication; and Feldman, *Wars of the Lord*. Vol. 3, p. 195, n. 14.) Davidson himself seems to have retracted this conclusion; see Davidson, *Rationalist*, p. 159, note 213.

beliefs in eternity were unacceptable, those of Plato *were* acceptable (although there was no demonstration [proof] to accept Plato's view – see previous paragraph). However, at the beginning of his discussion of creation, in chapter 13, Maimonides argued that "the purpose of every follower of the law of Moses and Abraham . . . is to believe that there is nothing eternal in any way existing simultaneously with God. . . ." (Pines, p. 285), i.e., that belief in *any* eternal matter, *even as did Plato*, was *not* acceptable for a "follower of the law of Moses." Therefore, if we are to take Maimonides at his word, that there are no actual contradictions in the *Guide*, only examples of subtle but intentional contradictions made by the author to conceal his true belief (see Maimonides' Introduction to the *Guide of the Perplexed*, the seventh cause; Pines, p. 18), we have to ask: What is Maimonides trying to hide? It cannot be belief in creation *ex nihilo*, because that is standard Jewish belief. Therefore, Maimonides' true belief (that he is trying to conceal) is creation a la' Plato; that God co-exists with eternal matter, and that He freely fashioned the Earth and heavens out of that matter, which is changeable, (thus) allowing for Divine will and miracles. This is also consistent with Maimonides insisting on proving God's existence irrespective of whether the world was created in time or not. (See above, Book Two, chapters 1–2.) Even if one does not believe this to be Maimonides' true position, it is undeniable that two of his philosophically minded, rabbinic intellectual descendants (Gersonides[70] and Ibn Kaspi[71]) held this position.

Chapters 26–31 conclude Maimonides' discussion of creation. In chapter 26 Maimonides cites certain rabbinic texts that might mean that God created the world out of pre-existent matter (bolstering Maimonides' likely true position; see the previous paragraph) and that the matter of heaven differs from the matter of Earth. An example of the former is a rabbinic text (Pirke de Rabbi Eliezer 3) that God created the heavens from the light of His garment (which might imply pre-existent matter), while an example of the latter is the rabbinic dictum (Genesis Rabbah 12:11) that "The creation of everything that is in the heavens derives from the heavens, and the creation of every-

---

70. YL Levi, *Peirushei HaTorah LeRabbeinu Levi ben Gershom*, Volume I: *Bereshit*, Mosad HaRav Kook, Jerusalem, 1992. pp. 22–3, 27–9. See also JJ Staub, *The Creation of the World According to Gersonides.* Scholars Press, 1982, pp. 47–61.

71. B Herring. *Joseph Ibn Kaspi's Gevia Kesef.* Ktav, 1982, p. 48.

thing that is in the [E]arth derives from the [E]arth" (Pines, pp. 331–2).

In chapters 27–29 Maimonides argues that the universe could continue to exist forever after having been created in time out of nothing, and that many expressions to the contrary (discussed mainly in chapter 29) can be interpreted figuratively. Also in chapter 29, Maimonides begins to discuss miracles, how they are "not permanent" (Pines, p. 345) and how certain rabbinic legends view them as having been built into the system from the beginning of creation, and thus they are not really "unnatural." For example, Rambam might argue that when the Red (Reed) Sea was created, it was created with the quality that it would split at a certain time. Thus, "[a]ccording to this opinion, the sign of a prophet (in this example, Moses) consists of God's making known to him [Moses] the time when he must make his proclamation [for the Israelites to cross the Reed Sea because it is about to split] . . ." (Pines, p. 345).

Chapter 30 is a complex chapter. It is partly lexicographic, defining words related to creation. For example, "earth" is an equi-vocal term, meaning both our planet (the sublunar world) and one of the four elements. In addition, Maimonides interprets Genesis 1 in light of his preceding discussion of creation[72] by addressing several theological and philosophical issues. Trying to keep Divine intervention to a minimum, he asserts that "everything was created simultaneously; then gradually all things became differentiated" (Pines, p. 350). In other words, the universe (whether created *ex-nihilo* or from pre-existent matter) was "brought into existence . . . by a single [creative] act."[73] The idea that God's creative process would require six separate acts on six different "days" was anathema to medieval philosophical thinking; therefore, philosophers reinterpreted the creation story in Genesis 1. The analogy used by Maimonides is that of farming. A farmer may plant several seeds at the same time which then sprout on different "days," in different stages.

Another issue that bothered many medieval philosophers, including Maimonides, was the idea of God separating the waters above and below the "firmament"/sky (*rakia* in Hebrew), because according to medieval philosophy water existed only on Earth. Maimonides cites a story from the Talmud (*Hagigah* 14b) in which there are stones of pure marble that give

---

72. Feldman, *Gersonides*, p. 213.

73. Davidson, *Rationalist*, p. 275.

the appearance of water; presumably Maimonides is saying that whatever is in the sky has the appearance of water[74] but is not water itself.

Maimonides, in continuing his discussion of water and firmament in chapter 30, mentions that this discussion contains "one of the concealed secrets so that the vulgar should not know it" (Pines, p. 353). Exactly to what Maimonides was referring is not known, but Crescas assumed it to mean that if the people felt that water and firmament were natural processes, they would no longer believe that God judges the world for rain on the High Holidays.[75] Maimonides concludes this chapter with some comments regarding Adam, Eve and the serpent, referring again to the fact that "only Seth was vouchsafed a true existence" (Pines, p. 357; see Book One, chapter 7). The section on creation fittingly concludes, as does the Biblical creation story, with a chapter on the Sabbath (*Shabbat;* chapter 31).

---

74. Davidson, *Rationalist*, p. 121, a "water derivative." In much ancient thought, however, the blue heavens were thought to contain water that was help up by a solid, dome-like structure referred to as the *rakia*, usually translated as firmament. See O. Fass, http://TheTorah.com/my-encounter-with-the-firmament, accessed 10/10/17.

75. Davidson, *Rationalist*, p. 124; Crescas in *Sefer Moreh Nevuchim LeHa-Rambam*, Part II, p. 60, note 50.

94

(3)

The next and last section of Book Two, chapters 32–48, discusses prophecy. This section is not as conceptually difficult as the previous sections on creation or the last section of Book One which discussed Kalam philosophy, but Maimonides here introduces a revolutionary notion regarding prophecy. As Maimonides himself says, it is similar to the approach he used with creation. He begins his discussion of prophecy with three different theories of prophecy and prophets. The first is the conventional "top-down" understanding of prophecy, that a prophet is someone chosen by God to deliver His message. The second, unconventional, understanding of prophecy is "bottom-up" – that morally and intellectually perfected human beings are able to "tune in" to the Divine, and thus obtain prophetic information. This is related to the idea of Divine overflow, discussed previously (e.g., Book Two, chapter 12); the information is all around us, but only the perfected individual is capable of "receiving" it. The third opinion is similar to the second, except that prophecy is not automatic; it allows for God to withhold prophecy from certain individuals. This latter idea is consistent with what we described as

Maimonides' secret position on creation from eternal matter (see Book Two, chapter 25) in that it allows for Divine will and Divine intervention (as in the Platonic model of creation).

Chapters 33 and especially 35 describe the unique prophetic character of Moses (see also Book Two chapters 37, 39 and 45 and Book Three, chapter 1). Chapter 34 discusses the way the people heard God's word at Sinai (via an angel). Chapter 36 emphasizes the idea that prophecy is related to Divine overflow (see also Book Two, chapter 12), mediated by the Divine active intellect, first through man's rational faculty and then through the imaginative faculty (Pines, p. 369); the latter "enables the prophet to predict the future."[76] However, if a prophet is not in the proper frame of mind ("sad or angry"), "prophecy . . . ceases" (Pines, p. 372). Prophets attain their high level of intellectual (and moral) perfection by detaching themselves from "bestial things . . . eating, drinking, sexual intercourse" (Pines, p. 371). The latter, of course, has implications for how Maimonides understood what

---

76. Feldman, *Gersonides*, p. 153.

happened on Mount Sinai,[77] during which time Moses did not eat or drink (e.g., Deut. 9:9).

Chapter 37 contrasts prophets with philosophers. Maimonides explains that the Divine overflow to philosophers (and scientists) is mainly to the rational faculty, while to prophets (other than Moses) it is also to the imaginative faculty, explaining why many prophecies are conveyed by example or parable. Chapter 38 discusses the qualities of prophets (e.g., courage, mental preparation, and the ability to speculate). Chapter 39 describes the unique quality of Moses' prophecies and how only his prophecies became binding law (Torah). Chapter 40 is a digression related to the purpose of law as leading to order in society, which will be an important theme of Book 3, and for Maimonides is a sign that Torah law is Divine in origin. Chapter 41 returns to the concept of prophecy and is another lexicographic chapter, defining the term "vision" and introducing different levels of prophecy (which will be detailed in Book Two, chapter 45). In this chapter, Maimonides refers to Balaam as a prophet (Pines, p. 386), but not Laban

---

77. I am indebted to Samuel Fleischacker for this insight. See his "Part 1 – Maimonides' views on Sinai and Prophecy" at http://thetorah.com/making -sense-of-the-revelation-at-sinai/, accessed 2/20/18.

or Abimelech (Pines, p. 387). Chapter 42 continues
the discussion of prophecy and angels. In this chapter
Maimonides again explains that every time the Bible
recounts a scene with an angel having been seen or
speaking, that scene is a prophecy or a vision, whether
this is explicitly stated or not (Pines, p. 358). This of
course implies that the stories of Abraham and the
three guests (Gen. 18), Jacob wrestling with the angel
(Gen. 32) and even the binding of Isaac (Gen. 22), (see
footnote 59) are all visions. Chapters 43 and 44 again
discuss prophecy in general.

Chapter 45 is a detailed description of the levels
of prophecy. Maimonides describes the two lowest
levels of prophecy, which he believes are really stages
preliminary to true prophecy – those of Divine in-
spiration (*ruach hakodesh*, in Hebrew), after which
there are five levels of prophetic dreams, which are,
in ascending order: where one "sees" a parable, hears
speech, sees a man, sees an angel or sees God; then
there are four levels of daytime visions, which are, in
ascending order: one seeing a vision, one receiving
speech, one hearing a man or one hearing an angel.
Maimonides concludes this chapter with another
description of Moses' prophecy, which was unique
in that it was without the imaginative faculty and

without the mediation of an angel. Along the way, Maimonides explains that Abraham at the time of the binding of Isaac (see the discussion above regarding Book Two, chapter 42) was addressed by an angel in a vision, which according to Maimonides is the highest level of prophecy, but is still a vision (see again, footnote 59). In addition, Maimonides clarifies the nature of Moses' prophecy by explaining that "Moses . . . heard from between the two cherubim, [i.e.,] without action on the part of the imaginative faculty [because the cherubim represent pure intellect – see Book Two, chapter 6]" (Pines, p. 403).

Chapter 46 continues the discussion of prophecy, giving several examples from the Bible. Maimonides concludes by saying "From what I have mentioned you may draw an inference to what I have not mentioned, for all these things . . . have occurred in a vision" (Pines, p. 406), meaning that Divine communication is always either a dream or a vision (again, see footnote 59). Chapters 47 and 48 conclude the discussion of prophecy and return to a few familiar themes: Chapter 47 reminds us that the Torah exaggerates (e.g. in Deut. 3:11, Og's height is described by telling you how big his bed was, rather than his actual height, which Maimonides assumes was about 2/3 the length of his bed). Maimonides also mentions that the extremely long life spans of the pre-diluvians (e.g., Gen. 5) were only of those exceptional individuals, not of the general population. Chapter 48 reminds us that whenever the Bible says God "did" anything, He did it *indirectly* according to pre-existing natural laws. (See also Book Two, Chapter 5.) Finally, Maimonides explains that all matter has four *characteristics* ("causes"): essential/natural (e.g., what we think of today as cause, as in cause and effect), those that relate to human free choice, those that are accidental (i.e., related to the matter's non-essential characteristics such as color) and those that are fortuitous ("random").

Introduction to Book Three

In the short introduction to Book Three, Maimonides says that he will begin the book with a discussion of the Account of the Chariot (*maaseh merkavah*) or Divine Science, named after the heavenly chariot seen by the prophets Ezekiel (mainly) and Isaiah. Even though these matters are generally not supposed to be taught or discussed, Maimonides was afraid that the "knowledge would perish when I perish . . . [which would be] extremely cowardly with regard to you [my favorite student] and everyone who is perplexed. It would have been . . . robbing one who deserves the truth" (Pines, p. 416). Therefore, at least "chapter headings" have to be taught (see below, Chapter 5). Maimonides also states that "no divine revelation came to me . . . nor did I receive . . . these matters from a teacher" (Pines, p. 416), perhaps opening himself to the criticism that this knowledge was not part of some ancient, hoary tradition (*mesorah*).

Book Three

(1)

The first 8 chapters of Book Three discuss Divine Science (the Account of the Chariot, *maaseh merkavah*). Both the prophets Ezekiel (1:1–28 and 3:12–14) and Isaiah (6:1–7) have a vision of God. It is mainly the vision of Ezekiel that Maimonides discusses in this section. A summary of that vision will be presented to better grasp what follows.

Ezekiel (1:1–28) describes the Divine throne surrounded by a radiance (*hashmal*), with each "leg" of the throne composed of a creature of human shape with four faces (a human face facing forward, a lion's face to the right, a bull's face to the left and an eagle's face to the back) and four human arms each with a wing attached (two wings modestly covering the creature's body and two wings spreading outward, each one of which joins the wing of an adjacent creature). Each creature's body tapers down to a single, round, unjointed leg that ends in a calf's hoof. Alongside each four-faced head was a free-floating double-wheel (one inside the other) of a rim of eyes that moved as the creatures moved, with the creatures always moving in the direction of the human face. Over the heads of the creatures was an expanse (the "seat"); over the expanse was a throne of sapphire upon which sat "the appearance of the figure of the majesty of [God]."[78]

In chapter 1 Maimonides asserts that the three non-human faces in each "leg" of the "Divine throne" are actually human faces that resemble those of a lion or an eagle, and that the face of the bull is really the face of a cherub (based on an analogous verse later in the book of Ezekiel, 10:20), i.e., that of a juvenile. Cherubs, of course, are important symbols of the Divine ecology[79] found in the tabernacle (*mishkan*) the Israelites built in the desert; cherubs were woven into the decorations of the outer tapestries that surrounded the tabernacle and adorned the top of the ark in the Holy of Holies where the tablets Moses received from God on Mount Sinai were kept, and whence Moses heard the Divine voice. As mentioned previously (Book Two, chapters 6 and 45), cherubs

---

78. Cf., M Greenberg. Ezekiel 1–20. Doubleday, New York, 1983, pp. 37–8.

79. I first heard this term from Rabbi Y. Poupko.

represent pure intellect, which is now linked to the purely intellectual nature of Moses' prophecy.

Chapter 2 explains that the motion of the throne "takes the direction that God had wished it to take" (Pines, p. 419), and "that the movers of the [detached double] wheels are . . . the creatures" (Pines, p. 421), signifying (again – see Book 2, chapter 19) God's active will at work in the universe; perhaps the eyes on the double-wheels (whose orientation to each other is not specified, but may have been perpendicular) symbolize God's omniscience. In chapters 3 and 4 Maimonides explains that the wheels represent the spheres of heaven, and the beryl stone that the wheels resemble (Ezekiel 10:13) is equivalent to the sapphire stone of Ezekiel 1:26 and Exodus 24:10 which signifies "the . . . matter of the physical world."[80] Beginning in chapter 5 Maimonides describes the three "apprehensions" (parts of the vision) of Ezekiel that require explanation: the wheels, the creatures and the "man" above the creatures; again, only "chapter headings" (i.e., outlines; cf. Book One, chapter 33) are explained (Pines, p. 426). Maimonides has already mentioned

---

80. Davidson, *Moses Maimonides*, p. 396, based on Book One, chapter 28 (Pines, p. 61).

that the wheels signify the spheres of heaven and that one of the creature's faces (the face of the bull) is really the face of a cherub – angelic beings that dwell with God, that represent pure intellect. Maimonides now asserts that these explanations will help explain the "man" on the throne above the creatures.

In chapter 6 Maimonides asserts that the visions of Ezekiel and Isaiah are similar (in that they both describe God sitting on a throne with winged angels).[81] In chapter 7, Maimonides tackles the "chapter heading" of the "man" on the throne, by emphasizing that the "appearance of the likeness of the glory of the Lord . . . is *not* the Lord" (emphasis mine) [and] . . . not the *Rider*, as He . . . may not be presented as a likeness [even] in a parable" (Pines, p. 430). Chapter 8 concludes this section of Book Three by discussing again the overflow from the Divine intellect to our intellects via the active intellect, the unique qualities of the Hebrew language, which is called the holy tongue, because it doesn't have words for matters related to the sexual act, and Rambam's first "explanation" of the purpose of the commandments – that they are

81. There are some differences as well. Isaiah's vision is not nearly as detailed (no flying wheels with eyes, no description of four faces, and no hoof-like foot) and the angels have 6 wings, not 4.

"intended to quell all the impulses of matter" (Pines, p. 433; see also Book Three chapter 33).

(2)

In chapters 9–25 Maimonides discusses providence. Chapters 10–12 discuss the origins of evil,[82] and explain how evil can exist in a world with an omnipotent and just God. Maimonides begins chapter 10 by introducing the idea of *privation*, that is, something that is a result of the human condition, such as hunger, illness, infirmity or death. It is not that God directly causes privations; rather, they are a necessary consequence of our having bodies made of matter. Chapter 11 discusses another potential source of evil, *ignorance*. Ignorance is the main reason for the evil that one person inflicts upon another, so this is a problem related to our fellow man, not to God. In chapter 12, Maimonides spells out in greater detail his understanding of the origins of evil. He explains that there are three kinds of evil: The first is evil which is inherent in matter (related to privation, discussed above); thus, because man is composed of matter, man suffers from certain "necessary evils." "The evils of

82. Halbertal, *op. cit.*, pp. 329–35.

the second kind are those that men inflict upon one another . . . [due to ignorance; see above]" (Pines, p. 444). "The evils of the third kind are those that are inflicted upon any individual . . . by his own action" (Pines, p. 445). Thus, there is no real evil in the world that can be attributed directly to an uncaring God. Moreover, the presence of evil does not imply a limitation on the power of God, but rather a consequence of the fact that we are formed from matter and have free will.

Chapters 13–16 expand upon these ideas. Chapter 13 deals with the meaning of life. Maimonides, in this and the following chapter (which deals mainly with medieval astronomy), rejects the notion of anthrocentrism – that the entire universe was created for humankind. For example, in chapter 13, Maimonides states that "the stars . . . do not exist for our sake . . . [but] to rule . . . over the night" (Pines, p. 454; cf. Gen. 1:17–18). In this chapter, he also defines the equivocal term "glory" as meaning His will when applied to God (see also Book One, chapter 64). In chapter 15 Maimonides again discusses the idea of "impossibilities" and why they do not limit God's power; again, God cannot do what is logically impossible in the universe as He created it (e.g., to have 2 + 2 = 5, as discussed in Book One, chapter 75 and Book Two, chapter 13). Finally, in chapter 16, Maimonides discusses the problem of *theodicy* – the vindication of Divine providence in view of the existence of evil in the world if God is just. This is of course related to the discussion of Maimonides' understanding of evil, above in Book Three, chapter 12. Similar to the way evil does not limit God's omnipotence, evil merely being a consequence of our being made of created matter and having free will, Maimonides will argue (in this section of Book Three and the next) that the existence of evil in the world also does not limit God's providence.

Chapters 17–24 are the "guts" of Maimonides' discussion of providence; the related topic of man's free will vs God's omniscience is discussed as well. Chapter 17[83] begins the main discussion.[84] In this chapter, Maimonides discusses five opinions regarding God's providence. He ascribes the first opinion, which is that there is no Divine providence because everything that

---

83. This chapter is called *Perek Hashgachah* – the Chapter of Providence by Maimonides' son in *Peirush Rabbeinu Avraham ben HaRambam Z"L al Bereshit ve-Shemot*, p. 18.

84. Halbertal, *op. cit.*, pp. 335–41.

happens is due to chance, to Epicurus. The second opinion, which he ascribes to Aristotle, is that God's providence is only in the heavens, extending down to the level of the moon, but not to the (sublunar) Earth, although the Divine overflow provides each species on Earth the faculties it needs to survive.[85] The third opinion, which we have already encountered (Book One, chapter 71) is that of the Asharite branch of Kalam philosophy, that there is no free will because everything is due to the will of God. The fourth opinion, which Maimonides ascribes to the other branch of Kalam philosophy, the Mutazilites, is that God controls "all details of existence except human actions."[86] *Maimonides'* opinion, the fifth opinion, is "the opinion of our Law" (Pines, p. 469), and a modification of the fourth opinion. This opinion is that man has free will, but that "divine providence watches only over . . . the human species and . . . is consequent upon the divine overflow" (Pines, p. 471), such that "providence is consequent upon the intellect . . ." (Pines, p. 474), and "is graded as their human perfection is graded" (Pines, p. 475). In other words,

---

85. Davidson, *Rationalist*, p. 153.

86. Halbertal, *op. cit.*, p. 337.

the more one is properly connected with God, the more Divine providence one experiences, and in Maimonides' view this is self-fulfilling. An individual very connected to God will work only to the extent that is necessary to support him or herself and his/her family; thus, for example, unnecessary business trips to unfamiliar locations during which a mishap might occur will be less likely.[87] This discussion continues through Chapter 17 and into Chapter 18. Similar to prophecy, providence also works from the "bottom-up" (i.e., it is the "spiritual achievement of one who seeks God")[88] rather than "top-down" (God watching over us).

Chapter 19 continues a discussion of God's knowledge that began in chapter 16 and continues through chapter 21, where Maimonides discusses the conflict between man's free will and God's omniscience, and argues that there is no deficiency in God despite the fact that He endowed us with free will. One way of resolving the conundrum between free will and God's omniscience is to argue (as did some philosophers[89] as well as Gersonides (Rabbi Levi ben Gershon; Ralbag;

87. I am indebted to my brother, Rabbi Jeffrey (Shalom) Katz for this example.

88. Goodman, *op. cit.*, p. 24.

89. Feldman, *Wars of the Lord*, Vol. 2, p. 76.

1288–1344)[90] that God's knowledge (and therefore Divine Providence) is general, not particular. According to this way of thinking, God does not know future particular events. This solves the conundrum of man having free will if God is omniscient, but seems to limit God's omniscience, and thus is rejected by most religious philosophers and theologians.[91] Maimonides also rejects this argument, calling it a "very aberrant opinion" (Pines, p. 462). Maimonides' argues instead in chapters 20 and 21 that God's knowledge is different from our knowledge (in other words, "knowledge" is an equi-vocal term; Pines, p. 483), since God is omniscient due to His Own complete internal self-knowledge, while we humans are of course not omniscient, and our very incomplete knowledge is external to ourselves. In ways not completely obvious (at least to me), this unusual definition of Divine knowledge allows for human free will and God's omniscience, according to Maimonides.

Chapters 22 and 23 begin the *Guide*'s discussion of the story of Job, raising the problem of theodicy – why

---

90. Feldman, *op. cit.*, pp. 80–84. See also the paradoxical statement in Chapters of the Fathers 3:19: "[Rabbi Akivah said:] Everything is foreseen, yet freedom of choice is given [to us]."

91. Feldman, *Wars of the Lord*, Vol. 2, p. 76 n. 4 and p. 140.

do bad things happen to good people in the face of Divine providence? Maimonides will also use some of these upcoming arguments for his discussion of the purpose of the commandments in the next (and last major) section (chapters 27–49) of Book Three.

A summary of the book of Job is needed to facilitate Maimonides' arguments in the following chapters.[92] The book of Job tells the story of a righteous sufferer. We know Job is righteous and is being tormented only because of a bet Satan made with God, as related in the book's prose prolog (Job 1–2). After a lament by Job (Job 3), the next 24 chapters of the book consist of poetic dialogs between Job and three of his compatriots (Eliphaz, Bildad and Zophyr), who each insist that if Job is suffering he must have sinned. Chapter 28 is a hymn to wisdom. Chapters 29–31 contain another speech by Job, followed by a speech by a new interlocutor, Elihu. Finally God appears out of the whirlwind (Job 38–42). The book's prose epilog (the end of Job 42) provides a happy ending.

In chapter 22, Maimonides begins by citing an opinion from the Talmud (*Baba Batra* 15a) that the

---

92. For an overview of the book of Job, see for example, VE Reichert, *Job: Hebrew text & English translation with an introduction and commentary*. Soncino, 1976, pp. xiv–xviii.

entire book of Job is a parable. Even if that is not the case, Maimonides argues, at least the first 2 chapters, which contain the dialog between Satan and God, "is indubitably, in the view of everyone endowed with intellect, a parable" (Pines, p. 486).[93] Maimonides further asserts, however, that the rest of Job is also a parable by pointing out a wordplay regarding Job's supposed place of origin, Utz, which Maimonides asserts is related to the phrase *utzu etzah* (Isaiah 6:8) which means "take council," i.e., "[m]editate and reflect on this parable [the book of Job]" (Pines, p. 487). Maimonides goes on to explain that Satan is the evil inclination (as well as the angel of death), but that Satan has no power over a man's soul; in fact, Satan is specifically told by God to spare Job's soul (Job 2:6). The soul, according to Maimonides, is what "remains of man after death" (Pines, p. 488) and what unites with the active intellect (see Book Two, chapters 6 and 12, and Book Three, chapter 27). Maimonides further explains that the "good inclination is . . . found in man when his intellect is perfected" (Pines, pp. 489–90). This relates to what Maimonides will explain later in

---

93. Maimonides also states that Satan is the angel of death, based on an opinion he cites from the Talmud (Pines, p. 489).

Book Three (beginning in chapter 27) that the purpose of the commandments is to perfect the body so that man can then seek intellectual perfection, and it is the intellectually perfected soul which unites with God after death in some way, as already mentioned. (See again the discussion below in Book Three, chapter 27). Maimonides also points out that Job is described as righteous, but not wise, otherwise "his situation would not have been obscure to him" (Pines, p. 487), as Maimonides will explain below in chapters 23 and 24. Maimonides also cites the well-known Talmudic legend that every Friday night when one returns home from synagogue, he is accompanied by one good angel and one bad angel, symbolizing the good and evil inclination; presumably Maimonides cites this legend to reinforce his interpretations of Satan as the evil inclination and Job's soul as representing the good inclination.

In chapter 23 Maimonides points out that "this kind of speech [i.e., blaming Job for his suffering] does not accord with the parable [i.e., what the book is trying to teach; see below]" (Pines, p. 492).[94]

---

94. Many opinions in the Talmud (*Baba Batra* 15a–16b) seem to blame Job for his suffering as well.

Maimonides points out, in quite an extreme fashion, how "health, wealth, and children" (Pines, p. 493) are not the ultimate goals of life. Maimonides then goes on to match each opinion in the book of Job with different opinions regarding Divine Providence that Maimonides outlined in Book Three, chapter 17, which can probably best be aligned as follows: "Job (before the revelation from God in the whirlwind) is in keeping with the opinion of Aristotle" (Pines, p. 494) that God controls only the heavens (the spheres) and is therefore not necessarily "just" or "merciful" in the (sublunar) world. "[The opinion of] Eliphaz is in keeping with the opinion of our law [as commonly understood, that Job must have sinned to deserve his suffering]"[95] (Pines, p. 494). "[The opinion of] Bildad is in keeping with the doctrine of the Mutazil[ites, that man has complete free will]" (Pines, p. 494) and "[The opinion of] Zophar is in keeping with the doctrine of the Ash[arites, that there is no free will]" (Pines, p. 494). Elihu, in Maimonides' view, represents the true understanding of the book, which is reaffirmed when God speaks out of the whirlwind, namely that we cannot fathom how God governs the universe, and

---

95. Gutmann *op. cit.*, p. 222.

thus "every misfortune . . . [should] be born lightly" (Pines, p. 497). Elihu might also represent the true view of Maimonides regarding individual providence working for those who deserve it.[96]

The very difficult idea – i.e., that God might purposefully allow a righteous person to suffer – is the subject of the very next chapter, chapter 24, which is called "the Testing Chapter" or "the Chapter of Trials (*Perek HaNisayon*)" by Maimonides' son.[97] This chapter discusses the equally troubling and related concept that God may test certain individuals out of love. One explanation regarding these trials that Maimonides rejects is that "God sends down calamities upon an individual . . . in order that his [ultimate] reward be increased" (Pines, p. 497). Maimonides disagrees with this approach because "this principle is not at all mentioned in the Torah" (Pines, p. 497). In addition, the calamities in this world cannot be to augment the reward in the world to come, because according to Maimonides, "the world to come is a natural result of life in this world,"[98] when the in-

96. Feldman, *Wars of the Lord*, Vol. 1, p. 41 and n. 22.

97. *Peirush Rabbeinu Avraham ben HaRambam Z"L al Bereshit ve-Shemot*, p. 324.

98. Halbertal, *op. cit.*, p. 331.

tellectually perfected soul unites in some way with an aspect of God (see the discussions in Book Three, chapters 22 and 27). Maimonides believed that "the aim and meaning of all the trials mentioned in the Torah is to let people know what they ought to do or what they must believe . . . a model to be imitated and followed" (Pines, p. 498). This applies to the binding of Isaac, which is to make "known to us the ultimate end to which the fear and love of God may reach" (Pines, p. 502) although again Maimonides reminds us that the "command [to sacrifice Isaac] came to him [i.e., Abraham] . . . in a vision" (Pines, p. 501).[99] Maimonides cites the episode of manna in the wilderness as proof that "those who wholly devote themselves to His service . . . are provided by Him with food" (Pines, p. 499). This section concludes with Chapter 25 which contrasts the actions of man, some of which are futile, vain and frivolous, with those of God, that are all good.

---

99. Maimonides does seem to say here that Abraham acted upon this vision, but as maintained earlier (footnote 59), it is possible that the entire episode can be explained as a vision. Maimonides would then mean that Abraham would have acted upon the vision, or did so only in the vision.

(3)

The last major section of Book Three (chapters 26–49) discusses the laws (or commandments) found in the Torah. The first half of this section (chapters 26–34), begins with a discussion of two categories of law found in the Torah – *chukim* and *mishpatim*. The first of these terms (*chukim*) is the plural of the Hebrew word (*chok*) which means engraved, and implies that these laws are etched in stone. The second word (*mishpatim*) is the plural of the Hebrew word (*mishpat*) which means sentence or judgment, and implies laws meted out by a court, or via a judgment. Traditionally, the latter are laws that have an obvious rationale (e.g., "thou shalt not steal") while the former are laws that have no obvious rationale, that are performed only because God commanded them (e.g., the dietary laws [*kashrut*]). Maimonides, as is his wont, will tweak this traditional categorization by explaining that the former are laws whose rationale is *easily* discerned, while the latter are laws whose rationale is not so obvious, because for Maimonides it would be ludicrous for God to require the performance of commandments that have no purpose. Maimonides explains further that while all laws have an underlying purpose, the particular details of the law may not. For example, some laws related to sacrifices (to which Maimonides will return in Book Three, chapter 32) were "imposed with a view to purifying the people" (Pines, p. 508), but, he goes on to say, perhaps with a bit of humorous hyperbole, that "no cause will ever be found for the fact that one particular sacrifice consists in a lamb and another in a ram and that the number of the victims should be one particular number. Accordingly, in my opinion all those who occupy themselves with finding causes for something of these particulars are stricken with a prolonged madness . . ." (Pines, p. 509).

In chapter 27, a key chapter in the *Guide*, Maimonides explains that the ultimate purpose of the commandments is to perfect the body and society so that one can be free of mundane concerns (e.g., safety or health) and be devoted to acquiring correct opinions and thus perfect his or her soul. Once one's soul is filled with correct opinions and perfected, it will be able to unite in some way with an aspect of God upon death.

In chapter 28, Maimonides makes the crucial distinction between necessary and true beliefs. *True beliefs*, as the name implies, are actually true. *Necessary beliefs* are those "necessary for the sake of political welfare" (Pines, p. 512). In other words, some beliefs are not actually true, but are necessary for society to properly function. An example of a necessary belief might be that God "responds instantaneously to the prayer of someone wronged or deceived" (Pine, p. 514). This belief, even if not true, may deter potential evildoers and therefore is necessary. As Halbertal points out[100] the more necessary (as opposed to true) beliefs one attributes to Maimonides, the more radical the *Guide* will seem.

Chapter 29 gives some of Maimonides' views regarding idolatry, in which Maimonides refers to a remnant of an idolatrous community which survived into Moslem times called the Sabians.[101] This group, mentioned in the Koran, claimed that some of their Arabic writings, such as "The Nabatean Agriculture" (Pines, p. 518) were actually translations of ancient works; this is presumably why Maimonides believed that their practices reflected those of idolaters who lived centuries earlier.

In chapter 30, Maimonides continues his argument

---

100. Halbertal, *op. cit.*, pp. 146–7.

101. Guttman, *op. cit.*, p. 222.

against idolatry by explaining that pagans believed that if they worship the stars, "the earth becomes populated and the soil fertile" (Pines, p. 522). "God . . . [in an effort to] efface this error from our minds" (Pines, p. 523), instead wrote in the Torah the exact opposite – that if we worship the "stars and the planets . . . [that] would be a cause for the rain to *cease* falling" [emphasis mine] (Pines, p. 523; cf. Deut. 11:16–17).

In chapter 31 Maimonides returns to the purpose of the laws of the Torah, first discussed in chapter 27. Here Maimonides adds that "every commandment exists either with a view to communicating a correct opinion, to putting an end to an unhealthy opinion, to communicating a rule of justice, to warding off an injustice, to endowing people with a noble moral quality, or to warning against an evil moral quality" (Pines, p. 524).

In chapter 32 Maimonides introduces one of his biggest bombshells. He explains that sacrifices have "no intrinsic religious value."[102] Rather, they were "a gracious ruse," instituted because ancient man had no other way of worship, and "a sudden transition from one opposite to another is impossible" (Pines, p. 526).

---

102. Feldman, *op. cit.*, p. 158.

"Through this divine ruse . . . the memory of idolatry was effaced" (Pines, p. 527). Maimonides argues that outlawing sacrifices in Biblical times would have been akin to the Torah saying today: "God has given you a law forbidding you to pray to Him, to fast, to call upon Him for help in misfortune. Your worship should consist solely in meditation . . ." (Pines, p. 526).[103] Maimonides acknowledged the radical nature of his assertion – "I know that on thinking about this at first your soul will necessarily have a feeling of repugnance" (Pines, p. 527). Rambam also adds that the reason sacrifices were limited to a central sanctuary was "to restrict this kind of worship" (Pines, p. 529).

In chapter 33 Maimonides continues the discussion of the purpose of the law from chapters 27 and 31, introducing another concept: the diminution of lust. "To the totality of purposes of the perfect law there belong the abandonment, depreciation and restraint of desires in so far as possible, so that these should be satisfied only in so far as this is necessary" is how Maimonides begins this chapter (Pines, p. 532). Finally, in chapter 34, Maimonides explains that "[t]he law was

103. The implication of this statement is that what is done today to worship God (praying, fasting, etc.) is also merely what people are used to doing, and may not really be as meaningful as silent devotion and contemplation.

not given with a view to things that are rare" (Pines, p. 534), which is a way to explain how the Torah could be generally good but that occasionally an individual might suffer. For example, theft is a sin even for the occasional kleptomaniac, who perhaps really cannot help him/herself.

Chapter 35 is the first chapter of the 2nd section of Book Three discussing Torah law (chapters 35–49), in which Maimonides explains that there are fourteen classes of commandments, each of which is discussed separately in its own chapter (chapters 36–49). Shem Tov[104] and Fox[105] both point out that even though Maimonides also divided all of Jewish law into fourteen categories in his classic compilation of Jewish law, the *Yad Hachazakah*/Mishnah Torah, the fourteen divisions used by Maimonides in the *Yad Hachazakah*/Mishnah Torah do not match those in the *Guide*.[106]

---

104. Shem Tov, *Sefer Moreh Nevuchim LeHaRambam*, Part III, p. 48a, first comment on Chapter 35.

105. Fox, *op. cit.*, pp. 28–29 and note 29 on p. 17.

106. Maimonides division of the law into 14 categories also differs from that of the Mishnah's six fold division. The Mishnah was the first topical collection of oral law, organized by Rabbi Judah the Prince in the early 3rd century of the Common Era. See the discussion in Davidson, *Moses Mai-*

Maimonides' outline of the commandments in the *Guide* begins the same way as does his great legal code, with laws related to the foundations of the Torah, which are the philosophical and theological underpinnings of religion (e.g., proof of God's existence, His unity, His incorporeality, etc.). These fundamental ideas need to precede any demands religion makes upon the individual. Maimonides also included laws in the *Guide* related to repentance and fasting in this first class of commandments, while he placed some of these laws (e.g., the Laws of Holy Days) in Book Three of the *Yad Hachazakah*/Mishnah Torah.

Maimonides' second and third classes of commandments in the *Guide*, those related to idolatry and improvement of moral qualities, are both included in Book One of the *Mishnah Torah*; this seems to be the single largest difference between the organization of the law in the *Guide* and in the *Mishnah Torah*. The rest of the differences are mainly in the ordering of the commandments. Maimonides' fourth through twelfth classes of commandments in the *Guide* correspond to Books seven, eleven, fourteen, twelve, three, two,

---

monides, pp. 212–215. Because the Mishnah included diversity of opinion, it is a collection, not a code of law.

eight, nine and ten of the *Mishnah Torah*, respectively. Maimonides' thirteenth class of commandments in the *Guide*, which includes laws regarding forbidden foods and the laws of the Nazarite,[107] correspond to parts of Books five and six of the *Mishnah Torah*. Finally, Maimonides' fourteenth class of commandments in the *Guide*, dealing with forbidden sexual unions, corresponds to Book four of the *Mishnah Torah*. Maimonides does not explicitly mention the contents of Book thirteen of the *Mishnah Torah* (Civil Law) in the *Guide*; presumably these laws would be subsumed under laws of property in class seven.

Throughout chapters 36–49 of the *Guide*, Maimonides provides rationales for many of the commandments. For example, magicians are put to death because they are idolaters; shaving the corners of the head and beard and certain mixtures[108] are forbidden because they are practices of idolatrous priests (chapter 37), and a large number of Torah laws are

107. A *Nazir* was a commoner who took a vow (usually for one month) to maintain him/herself in a higher state of ritual purity than was necessary (e.g., like a priest, s/he could not defile him/herself with a corpse; cf., Numbers 6:1–21).

108. E.g., the prohibition against using linen and flax in the same garment (Lev. 19:19, Deut. 22:11).

promulgated to wean the people away from idolatry, as is true for Maimonides in the case of sacrifices (see Book Three, chapter 32).

In chapter 41 Maimonides discusses the rationale for certain punishments. For example, he repeats the well-known defense of the rabbinic interpretation of *lex talionis* (e.g., an eye for an eye) as requiring only monetary and not actual physical restitution (the latter of which is what a literal interpretation of the biblical words would imply), by explaining that in most cases it is impossible to duplicate the exact injury in another individual, so that monetary restoration is the proper remedy.[109] He also explains why some crimes are capital crimes and some are not, and qualifies different categories of sinners (e.g., inadvertent versus deliberate).

Rationales for the Sabbath, festivals and some of their attendant laws are found in chapter 43, probably to combat the criticism of the concept of a day of rest which Romans thought was a waste of time.[110] In passing, Maimonides also mentions that many

---

109. Abraham Ibn Ezra (1089–1164) on Exodus 22:24 (long commentary), among others, makes the same argument.

110. Feldman, *Gersonides*, p. 217.

128

midrashim (legends) contain "poetical conceits" (i.e., poetic license) for the purpose of instilling certain "noble moral qualit[ies]" (Pines, p. 573) and thus are not meant to be understood literally.

In chapter 45, Maimonides returns to the topic of prophecy, explaining that prophecy occurs via the medium of an angel (via the imaginative faculty, and thus imagination plays a key role in symbolizing and concretizing the truths relayed to man's intellect from the Divine overflow; see also Book Two, chapters 6, 7, 12 and 45). Maimonides explains that it is because "the belief in . . . angels is consequent upon the belief in the existence of . . . [God] that . . . [God] commanded that the image of two angels (the cherubs) be made over the ark . . . [O]ne cherub . . . might have been misleading . . . [f]or it might have been thought that this was the image of the deity" (Pines, p. 577). Maimonides then explains several other features of the Tabernacle (and the later two Temples). For example, candles were "to glorify and honor the Temple" (Pines, p. 577). Modestly, Maimonides states that "for the table and the [show] bread . . . I do not know the reason . . ." (Pines, p. 578).[111] Similarly in chapter 47

111. Modern scholars would say these are to complete God's Temple, which

Maimonides will admit that he does not understand the reason for the law of the red heifer (used to atone for unsolved homicides; see Numbers 19).[112] Maimonides explains that hewn stones were forbidden on the altar for two reasons: "It is not fitting for that which shortens [human life, i.e., a sword] to be lifted up against that which prolongs it [i.e., the altar, by facilitating sacrifices which forgive sin,]" as well as the fact that "idolaters used to build altars with hewn stones" (Pines, p. 578). Maimonides also provides quite a utilitarian (and somewhat amusing) reason for the incense sacrifice – to improve the odor otherwise attendant to the daily slaughter and processing of so many animals. Maimonides maintains that various objects and people were anointed to sanctify and distinguish them from the mundane. Finally Maimonides explains that the ark was carried on the shoulders of the Levites, and not in a wagon (cf. I Sam. 6:10–15, II Sam. 6:3–8, I Chr. 14:7–11, 15:2) in order to exalt it.

In chapter 46, Maimonides returns to the topic of sacrifices (see also Book Three, chapter 32). He

---

was patterned after a residence.

112. Modern scholars would say that since (red) blood acts as a spiritual detergent, a red heifer's ashes, when mixed with its blood, adds to the blood's ability to purify.

explains that because "idolaters offered only leavened bread and made many offerings of sweet things and seasoned their favorite sacrifices with honey [so that it would taste good to the gods,] . . . [God] forbade offering up any leaven or any honey [on the altar] and commanded that salt always be offered [to show that the sacrifice didn't necessarily "taste good"]" (Pines, p. 582). Maimonides explains that the reason for roasting the paschal lamb is "due to [the] haste [with which the Israelites left Egypt]" "just as unleavened bread is [eaten on Passover to recall the] . . . haste [with which the Israelites left Egypt]" (Pines, p. 584). Finally, consuming blood was also an idolatrous practice and thus forbidden.

In chapter 48, Maimonides offers rationales for many of the dietary and related laws, e.g., a medical rationale for not eating certain parts of a sacrifice (such as the fat of the intestines or animal blood). Maimonides' famous speculation that eating meat boiled in milk was an idolatrous practice and therefore proscribed[113] is found in this chapter. Maimonides

---

113. See J Milgrom "'You Shall Not Boil a Kid in Its Mother's Milk': An archaeological myth destroyed", Bible Review 1 (3) (Fall 1985): 48–55 for the history of the understanding of Maimonides' suggestion regarding the possible anti-pagan polemical origin of this prohibition.

also discusses the ethical underpinnings of certain laws, such as not "slaughtering . . . [an animal] and its young on the same day" (Pines, p. 599; cf. Lev. 22:28) and "the commandment to let the mother go from the nest before removing the eggs or chicks (*shiluach ha-kan*)" (Pines, p. 600; cf. Deut. 22:6–7).[114] The chapter concludes with a medieval justification for a husband being able to annul the vows of his wife "[a]s women are prone to anger, being easily affected, and have weak souls" (Pines, p. 600), as well as an explanation of the concept of the Nazarite vow (see footnote 107): "it consists in bringing about abstinence from drinking wine, which has caused . . . ruin . . . [and because the nazarite vow] allows a commoner to be put in the same rank as . . . [a] high priest as far as holiness in concerned" (Pines, pp. 600–1).[115]

---

114. In *Mishnah Torah Hilchot Tefilah* – Laws of Prayer – 9:7, Maimonides disqualified the ethical underpinning of the law forbidding boiling a kid in its mother's milk, for otherwise why is eating meat permitted in the first place? Therefore, either Maimonides changed his mind when he wrote the *Guide* some years later and/or he was perhaps more prone to ethical underpinnings in his non-legal, more philosophical work, as per Fox, *op. cit.*, pp. 210–11 (although there are ethical asides throughout the *Mishnah Torah* as well).

115. Maimonides, though generally preaching moderation, can sound somewhat like an ascetic when it comes to some of the laws described

Chapter 49, a long chapter that concludes this section of Book Three, explains the rationales for certain other commandments. For example, prostitution is prohibited for several reasons: to prevent genealogy from being confused, to prevent "an intense lust for sexual intercourse and . . . constant preoccupation with it" (Pines, p. 602) and to prohibit letting "our thoughts range freely . . . to provoke sexual excitement" (Pines, p. 608). Maimonides mentions that certain laws, such as that of the levirate,[116] predate "the giving of the Torah" (Pines, p. 603).[117] Maimonides again explains (cf. Book Three, chapter 33) that some commandments are meant to minimize the "quest for pleasure" (Pines, p. 606). Maimonides intuits that sexual relations between close relatives is not biologically sound "for it would be . . . [like an] act that . . . [took] place between . . . [a] root and [a] branch" (Pines, p. 607). One reason for circumcision, Maimonides claims, is "to bring about a decrease in sexual

---

in this chapter and elsewhere. Again, I am indebted to my brother Rabbi Jeffrey (Shalom) Katz for this insight.

116. Levirate marriage is the now superseded practice of marrying your sister-in-law if your brother dies childless (Deut. 25:7–10).

117. That at least some aspects of levirate marriage precede the giving of the Law on Sinai is evidenced by the story of Judah and Tamar in Gen. 38.

intercourse" so that "lust that goes beyond what is needed . . . [is] diminished" (Pines, p. 609). Finally, again preaching moderation, Maimonides concludes that "sexual intercourse should neither be excessively indulged . . . nor wholly abolished" (Pines, p. 611).

(4)

Chapters 50–54 form an epilog to the *Guide*. In chapter 50 Maimonides explains some of the reasons for the narratives recounted in the Torah. For example, the stories of the flood and Sodom and Gomorrah are to teach that "[v]erily there is a reward for the righteous . . . and a God that judge[s]. . . ." (Pines, p. 614).[118] Maimonides also explains that we would understand more of the reasons for the laws whose rationales elude us today "if we knew . . . of the events that happened in those days" (Pines, p. 615).[119]

Chapter 51 (which Maimonides himself calls a "conclusion" – Pines, p. 618) contains the famous

---

118. Presumably Maimonides believed these were true (and not just necessary) beliefs.

119. This is similar to realizing how useful ancient near eastern texts are for understanding Scripture (e.g., J Berman, *Histories Twice Told: Deuteronomy 1–3 and the Hittite Treaty Prologue Tradition*. J Biblical Literature, 2013; 132 [2]:229–250).

"*palace parable*," in which Maimonides characterizes several types of individuals. Maimonides begins by describing a king who resides in his palace in the capital, and whose subjects seek him out. Some subjects are outside the capital city, others are inside the capital. Of those who are inside the city, some turn their backs to the palace, while others face the palace, but can't find it. Some find it, but can't find the door. Some find the door, and walk about in the antechamber, but not the inner courtyard. Some enter the inner courtyard and can be in the presence of the king, but can only see him from afar and do not speak with him. Finally, some try to see him, at least from afar, speak with him or at least hear him speak.

For Maimonides, those outside the capital are people without any true beliefs. Those in the capital who turn their backs to the palace are those with incorrect opinions. Those who face the palace but can't find it are "ignoramuses who [only] observe the commandments [without understanding]" (Pines, p. 619). Those who "have come up to the habitation and [just] walk around it" (Pines, p. 619) are "Talmudists" (according to the Ibn Tibbon Hebrew translation)[120] who "do not

---

120. Davidson, *Moses Maimonides*, p. 385; *Sefer Moreh Nevuchim LeHa-*

engage in speculation (philosophy)" (Pines, p. 619). Only "[t]hose who have plunged into speculation (studied philosophy) . . . have entered the antechambers [of God's habitation]" (Pines, p. 619). Note how Talmudic law is outside the palace, while philosophy is inside.[121] Finally, those who "have *understood* [emphasis mine] divine science [*maaseh merkavah*)] . . . have entered the inner court [of God's habitation]" (Pines, p. 619). *Prophets*, who are one step above philosophers, have "attained *perfection* (emphasis mine) in the divine science, [and consequently are able to] turn wholly toward God . . . [and] are present in the

---

Rambam, Part III, p. 64b. See also *Mishnah Torah, Laws of the Foundation of Torah* 4:3, where Rambam says that *maaseh bereshit* and *maaseh merkavah* are great things, while explaining what is forbidden and what is permitted are small things. Rabbi J B Soloveitchik, the consummate Talmud scholar, sought to defend Talmudists by arguing that Rambam meant that only non-philosophical Talmudists come up to the habitation and walk around without entering the antechamber (Kaplan, *op. cit.*, pp. 52–3), not that every Talmudist was non-philosophical. However, as there were well-known anti-philosophical Talmudists (e.g., Rashbah – see footnote 68, and related text; Rabad – see footnote 10, and related text; and Elijah of Vilna, 1720–1797, who famously stated that Maimonides' philosophy misled him [i.e., Maimonides] – see his comments to the Shulchan Aruch, Yoreh Deah 179:13), Rav Soloveitchik does not completely blunt Maimonides' critique of Talmudists.

121. Goodman, *op. cit.*, p. 158.

inner court" (Pines, p, 620). Presumably, they can at least hear God speak if not also speak with Him.

This chapter also discusses human perfection and how it can be achieved, and refines the idea of Divine Providence. Again, Maimonides emphasizes "solitude and isolation" (Pines, p. 621) as being conducive to attaining an apprehension of God[122] (see Book Three, chapter 32), and Maimonides gives some practical advice how to achieve this state during the recitation of the *Shema* prayer at bedtime when one is about to fall asleep (so-called *kriat shema al hamitah*, lit., the *Shema* [that is said] in bed). Finally, Maimonides returns to the idea of Divine Providence (see Book Three, chapters 9–25), explaining again that it is proportional to a person's intellect, and in many cases self-fulfilling, for when an individual is totally devoted to God, and cannot be distracted from that devotion, as were Moses and the Patriarchs, it will be much less likely that the individual will notice or focus on a misfortune that has befallen him or her (see also the previous, similar discussion in Book Three, chapter 17). Maimonides cites the Talmud (*Baba batra* 17a)

---

122. Maimonides' approach has been criticized as not involving any sort of communal activity – i.e., no need for *klal yisrael,* the Israelite collective; I first heard this argument from Rabbi G Bechhoffer.

that explains that the death of Moses, Aaron and Miriam "by the mouth of the Lord" (e.g., Deut. 34:5) does not mean "as God commanded" but that they died by a Divine kiss; Maimonides interprets this to mean "in the pleasure of [their] apprehension [of the Divine]" (Pines, p. 628). Maimonides ends this chapter by enjoining the reader to "multiply . . . those times in which you are . . . endeavoring to approach Him" (Pines, p. 628). Maimonides also explains that the perfected man need not fear death, because "when a perfect man . . . approaches death, this apprehension [of love of God] increases very powerfully . . . until the soul is separated from the body" (Pines, p. 627). Maimonides prepares us to be able to do this in chapter 52, explaining that the ruler of the palace represents God and that it is within our capacity to heed the active intellect and tap into the Divine overflow. Maimonides concludes the chapter by saying that love of God is achieved "through the apprehension of His being [to the best of our ability]," while fear of God is achieved by "[fulfilling] all actions prescribed by the Law [i.e., the commandments]" (Pines, p. 630).

Chapters 53 and 54, with which Maimonides ends the *Guide*, are also lexicographic/definitional chapters, so the *Guide* ends with the same style of chapters as it began. In chapter 53 Maimonides discusses two equi-vocal terms, *chesed* and *tzedek*. *Chesed* is defined as an excess of beneficence, and as it applies to God refers to God's beneficent act of bringing all into existence. *Tzedek* is defined as the way we perfect our souls with moral virtue, and as it refers to God in the way He judges the world with loving-kindness.

In chapter 54, Maimonides discusses the four different ways the word "wisdom" is used in Hebrew: apprehending true realities, acquiring moral virtue, acquiring the arts and using strategy. Maimonides also explains that man also has four perfections, elaborating on the discussion begun in Book Three, chapter 27: perfection of possessions (which Maimonides, unsurprisingly, characterizes as "the most defective" – Pines, p. 634), perfection of the body, perfection of moral virtues and perfection of rational virtues, which culminates in having true opinions about God (to the extent that this is possible) and in "permanent perdurance" (Pines, p. 635), i.e., unification (in some way) of one's soul with God (via the active intellect after death), which is unique for each perfected individual: "This ultimate perfection . . . pertains to you alone," thus allowing for some sort of individualized after-life (Pines, p. 635; see also Book One, chapters 41, 70 and 74.) Maimonides ends his great philosophical and theological work by explaining that "through assimilation of His actions" our "way of life . . . will always have in view loving-kindness, righteousness and judgment" (paraphrasing Jer. 9:23–24). Thus, while reaching for the pinnacle of human intellectual apprehension of God, Maimonides explains, there should always be intellectual energy for improving life on Earth (*tikun olam*), as we imitate God's loving-kindness and righteousness (Pines, p. 638), the highest form of ethics.

Acknowledgements

My first serious exposures to the *Guide* were from Dr. Albert Baumgarten and Moshe Lichtman (Meiri). I am indebted to my brother, Rabbi Jeffrey (Shalom) Katz for many years of helpful discussions and for a critical reading of an early draft of this work. Sadly, all errors are my own.

Annotated Bibliography

Editions of the *Guide*

M FRIEDLANDER. *The Guide for the Perplexed by Moses Maimonides*. Second edition. 1904. Routledge & Kegan Paul. There is a one volume edition which included all of Friedlander's footnotes (no date) reprinted by Hebrew Publishing Co. There is also an inexpensive Dover edition (1956) which did not include Friedlander's notes. Friedlander's was the first translation of the *Guide* into English. His introduction (and notes) are quite useful.

S PINES. *The Guide of the Perplexed: Moses Maimonides*. University of Chicago Press. Chicago and London. 1963. Two volumes. Introductory essay by Leo Strauss. Translator's introduction "The Philosophical Sources of The *Guide* of the Perplexed." The best translation of the *Guide* into English currently available. The introduction by Strauss is abstruse.

J GUTTMANN. *Maimonides, The Guide of the Perplexed*. Hackett. Indianapolis. 1952, reprinted 1995. An abridged translation. The introduction puts Maimonides' philosophy in the context of the history of religious philosophy.

144

Sefer Moreh Nevuchim LeHaRambam. Translated from the Judeo-Arabic by Shmuel Ibn Tibbon. Vilna 1904. Reprinted Jerusalem 1960, 2004. With the commentaries of Profiat Duran (ca. 1350–1415, **A**p**h**o**d**i =*Ani* [I am] Profiat Duran), Isaac Abravanel (1437–1508), Shem Tov ben Joseph ben Shem Tov (*Shem Tov*, 15th century) and Hasdai Crescas (1340–ca. 1410). [Hebrew]

Commentaries and Scholarship on the *Guide*

H DAVIDSON, "Maimonides' Secret Position on Creation" in I. Twersky, *Studies in Medieval Jewish History and Literature*, Harvard, Cambridge, MA and London, 1979.

M FOX. *Interpreting Maimonides: Studies in Methodology, Metaphysics and Moral Philosophy*. University of Chicago Press. Chicago and London. 1990.

LJ KAPLAN, editor. Maimonides: Between Philosophy and Halakhah: Rabbi Joseph B Soloveitchik's Lectures on the *Guide of the Perplexed*. Ktav and Urim. Jerusalem and New York. 2016. A topical commentary on some aspects of the *Guide*, compiled mainly from lecture notes from a course taught by Rabbi JB Soloveitchik in the early 1950's, in which Rav Soloveitchik attempted to put Rambam's philosophy in the *Guide* into the context of Rambam's other writings and into the Western philo-sophical tradition.

Books about Maimonides

HA DAVIDSON. *Moses Maimonides: The Man and His Works*. Oxford. 2005. A spectacular single volume of Maimonides' life and thought.

HA DAVIDSON. *Maimonides the Rationalist*. Oxford and Portland. 2011.

M GOODMAN. *Maimonides and the book that changed Judaism: Secrets of the Guide of the Perplexed*. Jewish Publication Society, Philadelphia. 2015. A single volume introduction to Maimonides' philosophy which I believe, finds more "contradictions of the 7th kind" than there actually are in the *Guide* and which in my estimation veers too far towards the mystical (see especially chapter 17).

M HALBERTAL. *Maimonides: Life and Thought*. Translated by J Linsider. Princeton University Press. Princeton and Oxford. 2014. Another very good, somewhat shorter single volume on Maimonides.

JL KRAEMER. *Maimonides: The Life and World of One of Civilization's Greatest Mind*. Doubleday. 2008. Also a very good single volume on Maimonides. Kraemer puts

STUDENT'S COMPANION TO *THE GUIDE OF THE PERPLEXED*

146

Maimonides into historical context, and provides much biographical information.

BZ BOKSER. *The Legacy of Maimonides. Philosophical Library.* N.Y. 1950. A short, well written introduction to Maimonides' thought, based mainly on the *Guide*.

Other Relevant Works of Scholarship

M FAKHRY. *A History of Islamic Philosophy*, third edition. Columbia. New York. 2004. Essential for understanding the philosophical background of the *Guide*.

S FELDMAN. *Gersonides: Judaism Within the Limits of Reason.* Littman Library of Jewish Civilization. Oxford and Portland. 2010. A terrific single volume introduction to Gersonides' (1248–1344) thought.

S FELDMAN. Levi Ben Gershom (Gersonides). The Wars of the Lord. Volume One. The Jewish Publication Society. Philadelphia. 1984. Volume Two. Philadelphia. 1987. Volume Three. Philadelphia. 1999. A masterful translation with useful introductions and notes.

G FRIEDLANDER. *Pirke De Rabbi Eliezer: The Chapters of Rabbi Eliezer the Great.* Sepher-Hermon Press. N.Y. 4th edition. 1981.

B HERRING. *Joseph Ibn Kaspi's Gevia Kesef: A Study in Medieval Jewish Philosophical Bible Commentary.*

Ktav, New York, 1982. This is one of Ibn Kaspi's (born 1279/80) few works available in English.

YL LEVI. *Peirushei HaTorah LeRabbeinu Levi ben Gershom,* Volume I: *Bereshit.* Mosad HaRav Kook, Jerusalem. 1992. [Hebrew]

J OBERMANN, L Ginzberg, HA Wolfson, eds. Yale Judaica Series. Volume I: *Saadia Gaon: The Book of Beliefs and Opinions.* Translated by S Rosenblatt. Yale University Press. New Haven and London. 1948, 1976.

M SHAPIRO. Changing the Immutable: How Orthodox Judaism rewrites its history. Littman Library of Jewish Civilization. 2015.

JJ STAUB. *The Creation of the World According to Gersonides,* Scholars Press, 1982.

HA WOLFSON. *The Philosophy of the Kalam.* Harvard University Press. Cambridge, MA and London. 1976. Extremely helpful for understanding their philosophy.

WOOTTON D. The Invention of Science: A new history of the scientific revolution. HarperCollins. New York. 2015. An intellectual tour de force.

Other Works by Maimonides

M HYAMSON. *Mishneh Torah: The Book of Knowledge by Maimonides.* Feldheim. Spring Valley and Jerusalem. 1981.

M HYAMSON. *Mishneh Torah: Book II: The Book of Love.* Bloch. New York. 1949.

These editions of the first two (of the 14) books of the *Mishnah Torah*, with Hebrew and English on facing pages were prepared from a manuscript that bears a note in Maimonides' hand attesting that it was corrected by comparison with his own copy of the *Mishnah Torah*.

P BIRNBAUM. *Maimonides' Mishna Torah (Yad Hazakah).* Hebrew Publishing Co. N.Y. 1967. A one volume abridgement and translation (with facing Hebrew and English pages) of the classic work.

E TOUGER. *Maimonides Mishnah Torah.* Moznaim. New York and Jerusalem. 1988–2010. A serviceable multivolume translation of the *Mishnah Torah* by a single author. (Yale Judaica series translations of all 14 volumes of the *Mishnah Torah* into English, each volume by a different author, are more scholarly.)

RL WEISS and C BUTTERWORTH. *Ethical Writings of Maimonides.* New York University. 1975. Includes the

Rambam's "Eight Chapters," his introduction to Chapters of the Fathers, or better Chapters of Principles (see Kraemer, Maimonides, p. 523, note 90; one of the 63 tractates of the Mishnah), which deals with comments about life and ethical matters.

F ROSNER. *Maimonides' Commentary on the Mishna – Tractate Sanhedrin*. Sepher-Hermon Press. N.Y. 1981. This includes Maimonides' introduction to chapter 10 of Sanhedrin (*Perek Chelek*), which discusses philosophical matters.

A HALKIN and D HARTMAN. *Epistles of Maimonides: Crisis and Leadership*. Jewish Publication Society. Philadelphia and Jerusalem. 1985. Contains the Epistle on Martyrdom, the Epistle to Yemen and the Essay on Resurrection. The first two letters were addressed to Jewish communities in distress; the last defends himself against charges of heresy, because of his seeming denial of bodily resurrection.

Index of Citations

Biblical

Talmudic

Mishnah Torah/Yad Hachazakah

Index

About the Authors

MOSES MAIMONIDES was one of the greatest Jewish minds of all time. Born in Cordova, Spain around 1135, his family fled from fanatical Moslem persecution. They passed through Fez, Morocco and Israel, eventually settling in Fostat (Old Cairo), Egypt. Also known as the Rambam, Maimonides became the leader of the Jewish community in Egypt for a time; he also studied medicine and became a court physician. He authored three great Jewish works (as well as many medical and scientific treatises): a commentary on the Mishnah, a code of Jewish law and his philosophical masterpiece, *The Guide of the Perplexed*. Published in 1190, the *Guide* has been translated into many languages and has had a profound influence on both Jewish and non-Jewish philosophers. Maimonides died in 1204 and was buried in Tiberias in Israel.

BEN ZION KATZ is a Professor of Pediatrics at Northwestern University's Feinberg School of Medicine and is an Attending Physician in the Division of Infectious Diseases at the Ann & Robert H Lurie Children's Hospital of Chicago. He is the author of over 70 original medical publications, as well as many book chapters and editorials on medical matters. He is also the author of *A Journey Through Torah: A Critique of the Documentary Hypothesis* (Urim, 2012) and has published many articles of Jewish interest in learned journals such as *Tradition, Jewish Bible Quarterly* and *Bekhol Derakheha Dehu* (Journal of Torah and Scholarship). He has taught for the Florence Melton Adult Education Program of Hebrew University, the Dawn Schuman Institute for Jewish Learning and Limmud Chicago, and has given invited presentations at meetings of the Association for Jewish Studies and the Herzl Institute in Jerusalem. He lives with his family in the Chicago area.